Focus

Straight-Forward Guide to Rediscover Your Concentration and Productivity Once Again and Master Your Success from Day One

2nd Edition

By

Rob Montgomery

The trademarks that are used are without any consent, and the publication of the trademark is without permission or backing by the trademark owner.

All trademarks as well as brands within this book are for clarifying purposes only and are the owned by the owners themselves, not affiliated with this document.

Table of Contents

Introduction

Procrastination is a phenomenon that happens to every one of us. One minute you find yourself doing your work, and the next you find that you're looking at e-mail or chatting on the phone with a friend. However, it's not the distractions that are making you late on your work, whether it is homework or something your boss needs within the next three hours. It's your brain telling you to stop doing something because it's too much for you to handle.

Just before you found something else to do, you may have experienced an increased heart rate, you were suddenly thirsty, or your palms grew sweaty. All of these signals are signs of stress happening within your body because you are mentally telling yourself you can't do whatever it is you need to get done. It could have been poor planning on your part or maybe your boss didn't allow you enough time to get this project done, but it's happened. You're now fifteen minutes away from your deadline and there is no possible way you're going to get it finished.

This reaction within our bodies is normal; however, it can be detrimental to our personal lives, careers, and education. The good news is, there are ways you can prevent this from happening. But first, you must look out for the warning signs in order to understand what you are doing when you are procrastinating.

Read on to find out the different warning signs you may be exhibiting that let you know you're already or you're going to procrastinate.

Master the Keys of a Stress- Free Organized Day

Being productive and efficient is an important attribute for a person to have in this society. Having both of these attributes means that you can get all of the work done and still not be stressed out and have time with your family. But finding ways to be efficient can be difficult, especially with all of the things that are going on in daily life. This guidebook is meant to provide you with 8 of the best tips that you need in order to stay focused and get the most done out of your day. You will learn how to use technology to your advantage, how to say no, and how eating the right foods and taking breaks throughout the day can really make the difference. Use this guidebook to get the right start on all of your work so you can get it done and go home happy.

Chapter 1:
Start Day off Right

The first thing that you need to do in order to be more productive in your day is to learn how to start the day off right. According to a study that was done at the Fisher College of Business at Ohio State University, those who are in a bad mood when they start out the day, whether it is because of a stressful commute, family issues, or something else, will have decreased productivity for the rest of the day. In many cases, this decrease in productivity will be as much as 10% for the day, even if they are working throughout. This means that if you wake up from the night feeling grumpy or you get mad right away in the morning, you are less likely to get as much done as you would like, even if you are trying to work hard. This is because your mind is going to be on other things rather than on what work is at hand.

If you feel like you are in a bad mood to start the day, you can take about 10 minutes and learn how to decompress. You can come up with any ritual that works for you, whether it is taking a few minutes to say hello to others in the office, dancing to one of your favorite songs, or looking at a funny video online. This is a good way to refocus your energy so that you can remain calm and a part of the bigger effort of the day. When your mind loses what it is angry about and instead focuses on something that is good, it will feel happier and you will then have more control over the things you are feeling. You will be able to concentrate on the daily tasks at hand and can handle any other stresses and distractions that are coming in during the day.

Chapter 2:
Take a Break

There is an unfortunate thought in America that everyone needs to be working at all times. They feel that the only way that they can get everything done is to work around the clock. This might seem like the only way to keep caught up, get everything done, make it to all of the appointments, and not fall behind. Unfortunately, this can often create the opposite effect in that you will have issues with concentrating and focusing the longer you are working without interruptions.

Americans have come under the belief that constantly working is the same thing as being productive. While you have no chance of being productive if you are not working at all, it is important to realize that unless the brain is working at its maximum capacity, you are not going to be getting as much of your work done as you think. Taking a break in between some tasks can make all of the difference. The break does not have to be anything special or last very long, but it is giving your brain a little recess to re-center and concentrate again.

Think of it this way, remember when you were a little kid starting out in school? You would spend a couple of hours inside learning new things, such as your letters and your numbers, and then right when you were starting to get tired or a little overwhelmed, you went out with the class for recess. Once you came back in you were no longer tired and you could take in more information and start new. This is the same idea when you are an adult. Taking a break is kind of like starting the rest button on your brain. It helps you to empty and refresh your brain so that you will have the energy and the room to fill it up again.

There are several ways that you can make sure to take breaks each day. The first thing, do not skip out on your lunch break. Most workers will grab something that is easy and eat it at their desk while working. This is not a proper break and is going to run you down faster than you can imagine. Take a step away from the desk and get a breather from the stresses that come with work; it is still going to be there when you get back. Other ways to get breaks include scheduling out other quick breaks as well. You can take out 15 minutes a few times a day and go take a walk around the block, read a book, or just stare out the window with something nice to read. It does not have to be anything that is difficult or that exciting as long as you give your brain the break that it needs. You will find that even with these quick little breaks, you are getting more done than anyone else during the day and feeling less frazzled when the day ends.

Chapter 3:
Make the Right Food Choices

Making the right food choices is almost as important to your brain as taking a few minutes away from the desk each day. Despite how important it is to your brain, many people will not even think about it. Millions of workers are spending their lunches eating processed, fast, and sugary foods that are easy to eat at the desk and in turn are making it impossible to be as productive as they should be during the day. The old adage "you are what you eat" is very true when it comes to increasing your productivity. The things that you eat during your lunch time will often determine how you are going to be feeling for the rest of the day; if you are eating these unhealthy foods you will feel lethargic and have trouble getting much done. On the other hand, if you choose to eat healthy and wholesome foods, you are giving your brain the recharge and fuel it needs to get so much more done in the afternoon.

You should take the time to consider the foods you are consuming during your lunch time. Salads and light sandwiches are great choices because they give you energy without the crash later on in the afternoon that can come with pastas, sweets, and coffee. It is also a good idea to supplement your light meal with a couple of healthy snacks throughout the day. This will help you avoid any slump that might occur when your body gets hungry and is worn out. Pack a baggie of carrots and an apple and eat one during the mid-morning and the other shortly before getting off from work. These will give you that extra boost so that you are able to keep concentrating on the work that is at hand rather than thinking about your hungry stomach or watching your eyes roll into the back of your head. Pair this snacking with a quick bathroom break or a walk around the office and you are getting two great things done at once.

When you are making your meal for work, you must make sure to avoid anything that is processed and heavy. This is going to cut out most of the processed foods that make lunch time easy for work. This is something that you will need to get used to; you will be able to make up your meal ahead of time at home or even prepare a mason jar meal to take with you. The heavy meal is going to make your body feel sluggish, even if you are eating several snacks throughout the day and all the bad things in the processed meal are going to make you gain weight. It is better to choose wholesome and healthy foods for your meals instead. If you are worried about staying full and satisfied during the day, make sure to create a quality lunch that is full of lean protein, water rich vegetables and carbs that are full of fiber. Some good examples of foods you can take for your lunch or snacks would include proteins like fruit and mixed nuts and have fish or chicken as the main thing for your meal. Stay away from bad ideas for food such as candy, cookies, and even pretzels.

You may be wondering why you should stay away from these processed and easy meals. Other than the fact that they are going to wreak havoc on your waistline, the way they work is going to make it impossible for you to stay productive during the afternoon when you are done eating. These processed foods will cause the levels of your blood sugars to spike really high before dropping, creating a quick energy boost in your body before forcing it into a slump that will make you tired. In many cases, once the slump hits, you are going to feel hungry again since your body is trying to get the energy back. Avoiding foods like these will keep your energy levels up so that you are rejuvenated and not feeling tired and even more hungry in the long run.

Chapter 4:
Be Flexible

If you want to get a lot of things done in the day, you need to realize that flexibility is all a part of it. Have you met those people who will not have any flexibility in their schedules at all? They might make a list of things they want to get done during the day or the week and that is exactly how things have to be done. There is no room for error and if you are not on their schedule way in advance, they have not time for you. Do you remember how these people were? They are constantly running around with their heads cut off. When someone at work or in their family asks if they can squeeze something else in, they go crazy and might not be able to handle the extra pressure of veering from their list. They might be running around a lot, but it is easy to tell that they are really not getting that much stuff done each day.

While this might be a little too extreme for most people, it is used to illustrate how important flexibility is. That is not to say that you should just throw away the to-do list and just sit around doing nothing. It is important to have this list because it can help you to see what things need to get done; the important difference is that you also need to realize that things are going to change throughout the day and you have to be ready to keep up with them. Sure, you might have a few things that you need to get done, but your son needs you to go and drop off some homework, or there is another little project at work that needs to be done first in order to make other tasks on your list easier. Things are always changing in life and you need to be flexible to keep up with them if you want to get ahead.

Making a list of the things that you want to do each day is one of the best ways to stay on top of the things that you need to do. The important thing that you need to keep in mind is that you cannot let that list make you inflexible. According to the author of "Wicked Success is Inside Every Woman, "A lot of people feel that their day's been wrecked if they have to change their plan, but the most effective people understand that's part of the job. I always start my day with a plan, but by 9 a.m. I've busted that plan."

The plan that you have for the day is more to be taken as an outline instead of something that has to be done or else. You can work hard to get the things on the list done, but also save some room in case other things come up and you need to try and fit them into your day. You are not going to be too efficient in your life if you are avoiding important projects just because they are not on your schedule, especially if a particular project has to be done first in order to make the projects you have work.

The first thing that you should do is make out a master list. This can be pretty simple to do. Take a look at all of the things that you would like to get done in the day and just write them all down. Now, take the time to figure out which ones are the most important and need to get taken care of right away. Do you need to go over your notes before the early morning presentation or edit a paper that isn't do for a week first? This is pretty easy to see which one you should do first. Go through your list of things that need to be done and use highlighters to sort them out; one color for things that have to get done first, another for things that should still get done that day if possible but are not quite as important, and then another for things you would like to get done but which could wait for the next day. This organization will help you to see clearly which things you must get done during the day and can help to get some of the clutter out of your head so that you can concentrate more. Then, go down the list in the order of most importance, adding in more things and color coding as the day goes on. With this list, when the day ends and before going home, take the time to make a new list for the day before. Start with the things that you did not get done today and place them onto the board, adding in other things that have come up throughout the day as well as anything new that might be important for the next day. Getting this all laid out before you go home will allow you to take a breather once you are off instead of spending the whole night worrying about what all needs to get done. This will give your brain a rest so that it is able to think clearly and more efficiently tomorrow.

Even with the list, you need to take the time to realize that things happen and you must be flexible. The list is a tool to stay on track, not something that must be abided at all times. For example, if your boss gets sick and you have to present to the stock holders that day, getting prepared and completing that tasks needs to be more important than the other things on your list. Having this flexibility to change things around will make it easier to be productive and get your whole list done.

Chapter 5:
Use Technology for a Purpose

Technology is a great tool that can help you to get a lot done in your life. You can send out emails in seconds, look up information, pay bills, and keep in contact with those you love all without leaving the couch. Some people have even begun to work from home because it is so efficient, provides a lot of opportunities and has flexible hours for the family. With access to technology at all times, it can sometimes be hard for people to get a handle on their technology use and this is where a lot of people are going to find that their productivity goes away. It is almost impossible to get anything done if you are going to spend all day looking at videos or pictures online or you are just watching movies.

This does not mean that you are going to have to avoid technology all of the time; in fact, doing this might be impossible. Technology can be a great tool that can make your life easier, but you have to develop some discipline about when and how much technology that you are using. It is often recommended that you set about15 minutes increments for being online, to look through your social networks and that is all that you get. If you find that you are at work perusing through websites that have nothing to do with work, you are most likely not being that productive. Google chrome has a website blocker that will completely block you from looking at certain websites so you do not get distracted.

For those who are not looking to get that extreme, there is also the option of blocking you out of certain websites during certain times of the day. This can be nice because it will make it so that you are not able to get online during work hours, but you can still see the things that you want when at home or on the weekends. Social media is not the only thing that could be causing issues when it comes to technology, you also need to watch out how much time that you are spending on email. If you are checking work email, that is fine since you will want to be kept up to date on what is going on in the office. Personal email can also be fine if you are taking a break in between the tasks that you are trying to complete. The issue comes when you spend an hour on your email or you are looking back and forth at it every few minutes rather than doing your work. At times, your work email can also get distracting. If you get an email from another office that seems confusing or you have a lot of questions about, take the time to call them. A few minute phone call can usually clear it all up rather than spending all day sending emails back and forth.

As mentioned, technology is a great thing to have in your life. It can make it easier to get things done and will even organize different aspects of your life. It is just important that you take a step back and only use technology when it is needed; let it help you out in your life rather than distracting you.

Chapter 6:
Balance of the Workload

Balancing out the work that you are doing throughout the day can often make a big difference in how you are getting things done. Each of the tasks that you accomplish during the day will require a different amount of time as well as different levels of your concentration. If you are able to do it all the right way, you will be able to use this to your advantage. This balancing act can sometimes be difficult to accomplish though. For example, if you spend all day working on one project, you might have got a lot done, but it is not going to feel that way. On the other hand, if you are spending all day on small little tasks, you will be surprised at how much you have left to do.

In order to use the balance of your workload to our advantage, you should start placing and identifying the tasks that you must complete into two basic categories; intensive work and weeds. Weeds are the small and easy to accomplish things that you will be able to get done in no time such as minor organizational tasks, phone calls, and dealing with emails. Intensive work is anything that is going to require your concentration for an extended period of time, such as a large project, a report, writing, editing, management tasks, and preparing a presentation. You need to learn how to balance these two types of work so that you are getting them done effectively.

For the most part, you are going to be able to get the weeds done in no time. While they are not going to take much effort or concentration on your part, they are still things that must get done in order to perform your job. One way that you can handle these is by getting them all out of the way when you first walk into the office in the morning or when you first wake up. Check all of your messages, read the emails, and then get them handled as soon as possible. You will then be able to spend the rest of your day concentrating on other things that are going to take up more of your concentration. With the little things out of the way, you are not going to need to worry about the other things and can give your full concentration to other important tasks.

Another way that you can balance your activities is to use the weed tasks as little breaks during the day. You could spend an hour or so on one of your more important tasks and then take a few minutes to rest your mind while replying to emails and answering phone calls. Going back and forth between these tasks provides you with an opportunity to get things done, gives your mind a break, but still allows you to get the important tasks done on time.

Chapter 7:
Perfectionism is Not Perfect

People are under the impression that they have to get everything done to perfection. They might spend hours working on a project, just to get it perfect even though it has been a great project for quite some time. This perfectionism might show how dedicated you are to the job, but can make it really difficult to get anything else done throughout the day. If you are spending a week on just one project, hoping to get it perfect, you are not going to be getting all of your other tasks done and your productivity is going to go out the window in no time. It is better to do a great job on a task and the move on to one of the others that you need to get done, rather than concentrating too much and wasting too much time on just one project.

Perfect work has been a thought that is encouraged since little kids went to kindergarten. If not properly managed, this thought process is going to be very counterproductive and make it difficult to get things done. It is a good idea to pick your battles and learn how to just accept the hard work you have done. This can be even more difficult for women who are known to be perfectionists.

This does not mean that you shouldn't put your best foot forward on all the projects, but if you find that you are strapped for time, prioritization will have to come in. Compromise a perfect job on a project with a great job on that same project and finishing up on another one. For example, if you are just sending out an email to a co-worker, you do not need to read over it three or more times. Just read it once with spell check and send it off so that you are able to get on to the next email or the next project.

There are a few areas where you might find that using perfectionism can help. If you are working on an important presentation or creating a new brochure for the company, go ahead and take your time and be perfect. This is where the balancing can come in as well. If you saved time on that email to your coworker by not rereading it over and over, you are going to have the time needed in order to perfect the larger project that deserves more of your attention.

Chapter 8:
Learn How to Say No

Learning how to say no to someone, especially if that person is your boss, can be really difficult. Everyone is worried about impressing others or they do not want to lose their jobs in the rough economy. They will sit there and take on more and more work in order to look impressive and get everything that looks important done. Soon they have too much on their plates and they are either not going to get it all done in time or they will not perform the tasks the way that it should be done.

It can be really easy to take on too much and become overwhelmed and distracted at work or in your life. One of the best secrets that highly productive people have is that they know when and how to say no to people. This can mean two things; saying no to more work and saying no the distracting people, the complainers, and the whiners who get in the way. If you are going for the second way of saying no, you can try out this little activity. When you are trying to get things done during the day, bring some headphones with you and put them on. This will send out the message to others that you are busy and you will also be drowning out the noise around you.

The second one, learning how to say no to people and more work, can be really difficult. You will need to explain how you already have too much going on right now and you would not be able to give it the right attention that it deserves. When it comes to your boss, you must be firm, but still tread lightly. A firm no is not always necessary either. Instead, you can ask the boss to prioritize the tasks that they think are the most important given what you are already doing. This will force the boss to understand the situation better and gets them on your side. You never said that you would not do the task, you just showed the boss how much you are already there for the company and helped to realize that there is already too much going on.

Saying no to tasks can be tricky, but you have to learn when your plate is getting too full. Take a step back and recognize everything that you are already doing and be realistic about how much you have to take on. If you take on a project that you do not have time for, you will become less efficient because you will be worried about everything else and will not be focused. Take on only the tasks that you are sure you can complete; if you end up with more time when you are done, it is fine to take on a few more things later on.

Create Routine & Strategy

Chapter 1:
Creating a Routine

Your mental organization skills are just as or even more important than your physical organization skill sets. In order to be a physically organized person, you first must have a routine in order to keep your life organized. Routines are comforting, familiar, and they put us in a productive, good mood.

Perhaps you like to get a cup of coffee every morning or you eat breakfast at a certain time. These small things are all part of your daily routine, and by changing some of what you do during the day can keep you from creating more clutter in your home. Our routines are made of habits. And habits can be changed and broken.

Habits

It's amazing how such a small word plays such a huge role in our lives. Habits fuel routines and routines the course of your life. A habit, for good or bad, once formed becomes an integral part of us.

As such, it is difficult to form new habits as it requires a conscious and intentional change, a dismantling of the former habit that is being replaced.

A habit can only be fought with a habit. Most experts agree that it takes between 21 and 30 consecutive days for a repetitive action to become a habit. Following this timeline you could establish 17 new habits a year. Just think of the transforming power 17 new good habits would have in your life.

When forming a new habit it is important to have a constant reminder that prompts you to your new habit. Stick with it for the entire course of 30 days. The first few weeks will be the hardest but it will become easier each day.

Many interviews and studies have compiled popular habits of highly successful people. These habits include:

- Waking up one hour earlier to get more done,
- ✓ Minimizing distractions
- ✓ Getting enough rest
- Eating a healthy breakfast
- Prioritizing their day and eliminating with the dreaded task by completing it first.
- Finding their time valuable

Decision-Making Process

In order to be a productive individual who is organized mentally, you must be able to make decisions. Decision-making is a difficult process for some and should not be taken lightly. However, a lot of people spend hours upon hours agonizing over a decision.

Rather than do this, you should set a deadline for any important decisions and make others in a reasonable amount of time. For instance, if you need to decide where your child is going for summer camp, make sure you set a time limit of a week to decide so that you have adequate time to research facilities.

If you need to decide what you're going to eat that night, make your decision within sixty seconds. It will make life a lot easier.

In addition to setting a deadline for decision-making, you'll need to identify what the most important factor is with your decision. It might be convenience, price, practicality, time, or anything else you deem important in the decision-making process.

That is what you need to focus on rather than any other aspect of the decision. So, for example, you know you need a new cell phone. A good way to narrow it down is to decide how much you can afford and go from there. Don't bother looking at phones that are over your price cap.

To-Do Lists

When you're making a to-do list to keep your day organized, make sure to keep it brief and give yourself no more than five tasks. If you're spreading yourself too thin throughout the day, you're going to forget about staying organized and move from one task to the next while leaving clutter in your wake.

A good way to stay focused on your tasks is to list five of them on an index card in large, bold letters. Complete those five tasks and then turn the index card over and put five more on the back.

By doing this, you will be able to feel less stressed and focus on what you are doing rather than what you need to do several days in the future.

Another creative way to create a five point list is to use a rotating goal list. This is simply pretty sheet of paper with 6 post-it sized boxes printed on it.

The first box is for the day's date, and the rest for specific goals. To use this rotating goal list peel of a post it note, write your goals and place them onto into these boxes.

The advantages of this method is that it is visually neater than crossing of items on a paper. Once the task is completed, simply peel of the sticky note and throw it away. They can easily be replaced and rearranged based on priority.

For this you can designate the first box to the most important task, followed by the others. You can also use different colored post it notes. This method is much more visual and it is fun to peel off the accomplished sticky note task. Many find this method very motivating and fun.

When creating your to do list remember to clearly define your goal. Do not leave it vague or undefined. Make sure the goal is attainable and measurable.

Extinguish Hyper Focus

Setting alerts throughout the day on your phone, computer, or even a kitchen timer will help pull you out of a hyper focus state. A hyper focus state is when you are so focused on what you are doing at the time that you lose track of how long you've been doing it.

You might find you're perusing the internet for information and end up logging onto a social media website or bidding website. Before you know it, you've spent more than an hour on that website where you should have been doing other work.

This messes up your routine and makes you feel stressed, which leads to you forgetting about organization, either mental or physical.

Say 'No'

For some of us, it's very difficult to say no to coworkers, bosses, loved ones, friends, and even strangers. It's best to know your limits when it comes to doing things for others and understand that it's okay to say no if you have to.

People will have more respect for you and they will learn your boundaries. If you're someone who says 'yes' to everyone, stop spreading yourself too thin and begin to politely tell others that you are unable to help them with their task.

Use simple phrases such as, "I'm sorry but I can't do this right now." True friends, loved ones, and polite individuals will understand and respect it. With those who continue to push, you will need to be firm and simply change the subject.

It is ok to be vague and simply say it does not fit your schedule. You do not owe anyone a detailed explanation. It is your life and you need to safeguard your time for what truly matters.

If you have a soft personality and find it difficult to answer no directly or you are unsure simply let them know that you need some time to think about it. Then take the time to look at your schedule to see if it is feasible.

You don't have to say 'no' to helping your kids do homework or to helping your significant other with a project, but make sure that it's in your schedule if it's important. If you find that you are pressed for time but are interested in helping offer to help-out in another way.

Plan Your Day the Night Before

Life can get hectic, but you can help alleviate some of the stress and be better organized by planning your day out ahead of time. If you need something specific for an appointment, work, or your kids, be sure to set it out the night before and put it in a place you will remember.

Make lunches the night before and set them in the refrigerator in a lunch box and put your keys on the hook by the door so that you know where they're at in the morning. By doing this, you will feel less rushed and you will be less likely to forget things.

Make Time for You

This is your number one way to reduce stress and get organized in your life. If you're not making time for you, getting organized will be too overwhelming for you. This doesn't mean that you need to make time for organizing or doing errands.

It means you have to make time for you to relax such as thirty minutes to read a book or play a game. It has to be something that makes you feel relaxed and helps you get rid of stress; otherwise, you will easily become overwhelmed.

You've started with organizing yourself mentally; now let's get to how you can organize items within your home to make your life easier and less stressful.

Get it DONE

Let's face it. A lot of times, you may feel like you're not doing much in your life. You may feel disgruntled, frustrated, and even hopeless with how things are going on. If you're not happy with where your life is headed, the good news is, you have all the opportunities to change its direction. Don't just sit back and imagine what your life can be. Take that step and turn it into the life you've always wanted.

And this is what this book aims to do. It's not just going to teach you how to manage your time or improve your productivity; it's going to inspire you to put order back into your life.

This book contains proven steps and strategies on how to live the life you've always wanted. From changing up your perspective on work to jumpstarting your productivity, you'll learn all the tricks on how to get things done. You don't have to second guess yourself about making that change any longer. With the right guide, you can set yourself up for success in a few easy steps.

Thanks again for downloading this book, I hope it helps you become the best you can be.

Chapter 1:
Conditioning Your Mind to Get Things Done

This modern world puts a lot of pressure on being productive. This is because there is often a direct correlation between how much you work and how much you will be paid. If you are the average person working 48 or more hours a week, you're probably feeling overwhelmed by the list of tasks that you need to accomplish at work daily. In fact, at the end of the day you may find that you have accomplished less than half of what you had in mind. In the quest to do more and earn more, your whole existence has turned into a cycle of stress.

Stress can wreak havoc on all aspects of your life. It's not just your career, but it can also affect your personal relationships, and how you enjoy your life. Stress can kill your productivity and even rob you of happiness and fulfillment. This is why conditioning your mind to minimize stress and maximize productivity is important if you want to achieve more. In order to become more productive, you need to start with the mind.

Most people don't understand that stress is really more a thought in the brain, rather than a state of being. This means that you have a choice over stress. It may not seem like you have control, but you do, and you don't even realize that you have this power. Against all popular belief, you actually have more time in your hands than you make yourself to believe. You can finish everything you need to do for the day, and still feel like a superhuman productivity machine. The only thing holding you back from realizing that is you.

Relax, don't do it

The first thing that you need to do to condition your mind for better productivity is to take some time out to clear your mind.

If you feel you don't have time for that, then you should make time for it. Getting your mind in the zone takes practice, but once you have that focused calmness, and you're in a state of relaxed awareness, you'll be able to do more, and not feel the load.

One of the things that you can do to stop stress in its tracks is to learn how to pick your battles. Don't just take on every single task that comes your way. You need to narrow it down to what's really important. Even though, it means to say "NO" to some people.

When you allow people to interrupt you, your mind suddenly loses its momentum in the current task to adapt itself to the new concern being presented. It takes time for your brain to readapt to the context of the new problem so even though you think you can handle it all at once; you're actually setting yourself up for more stress.

Take a Firm Hold of your Subconscious

Your mind is making a countless number of decisions today, with many being made in your subconscious. How you can tell that a decision has been made in your subconscious is through evaluating the resulting behavior. Should you find, yourself behaving differently than normal, our subconscious mind is often at work.

Take for example you are working towards driving to the office. Your mind is on the presentation that is due in one hour. You were hoping to get to work early enough to polish off. Normally, you are a happy, and understanding person. However, on this morning, you are nervous and anxious, and stuck behind slow moving vehicle. You then transform into an entirely different person and become abusive and rude to others in the traffic. It seems as though your mind has run away with you and your unconscious, generally silent mind, has taken over. This change in behavior is not helpful to you or your life, and that is why you need to condition your mind.

Taking a hold of your subconscious requires you being aware of what you are thinking, so much so that you are able to make the decision to pause and think through an action before you even carry out some movements. You can condition your mind to understand what lies hidden within you, which in turn can help you rid yourself of negative thoughts or voices inside of your head. This can be accomplished by simply increasing your awareness to your thoughts. Before your thought turns into a certain behavior, you can make a conscious decision to change your mind.

Meditate

It may seem counter intuitive to take time out of your day to just sit there and be one with your thoughts, but meditation is actually one of the most effective ways to condition your mind to do more. Meditation retrains your mind so that it's able to focus on just one thing at a time. Learning how to focus for longer time periods can help your cut back on all the distractions. Once you become more focused, it will be easier for you to retrain your brain to engage with itself to get more things.

Developing focus through meditation takes time so don't get discouraged if you feel you're not getting anywhere in the first few days. Just keep at it and pretty soon, your body will begin to catch up with your relaxed state of being.

Start off by committing just 5 – 10 minutes of meditation a day. There are a lot of ways to meditate, but don't stress yourself too much about finding that perfect method. Your goal at this point is to turn it into a habit.

Set a time and trigger for this. Whether you prefer to meditate in the mornings, after brushing your teeth or in the afternoon while taking your break, you need to consciously incorporate it into your routine until it becomes a thing.

Find a comfortable and quiet place where you can meditate in peace. It can be your room, that hidden spot in the park, or that quiet corner somewhere in your office, as long as it buys you a few minutes of not being bothered by anything or anyone.

Be comfortable and concentrate on your breathing. Close your eyes, slowly breathe in through your nose and exhale through your mouth. Stay focused on your breaths by counting them down. If your mind starts to wander, and it will at first, bring your focus back to your breathing. With a bit of practice, you'll get better keeping still in no time.

Understand your Emotional Pay Off

When your mind makes a decision, it is often because there is some sort of pay off that you will receive. If you choose to eat a meal, the payoff is you will no longer feel hungry and will be able to complete other tasks more effectively. Should you choose to try to complete too many tasks in one day, the payoff could be that you will feel a sense of accomplishment or pride in being able to finish off your to do list. There is always a reason that you are making any decisions, and the reason often directly relates to a change in your emotional state.

Once you are aware of why you are carrying out certain actions, you can condition your mind to attach a particular meaning to those actions that you are not willing to do – basically improving on their emotional payoff.

In this way, you will be able to get more things done, especially when you are dealing with tasks that are unappealing, or that you would prefer to procrastinate and move forward. Changing their emotional payoff means that you will be able to finish them faster and much more efficiently that you had previously considered.

Chapter 2
Setting the Right Goals to Get Things Done

One of the biggest mistakes that people tend to make when trying to increase productivity is that they try to pack in as much activity as they can into their to do list. From simple everyday errands to larger scale projects that last for years, suddenly it becomes a race to how much you can accomplish within the set time. You may be able to accomplish a lot at first, and believe me it will feel amazing, but once the initial excitement passes, you might find yourself tired, burnt out, or just daunted by the insurmountable work on your plate. When you fail to set attainable goals for yourself, you set yourself up for failure.

Improving your productivity and getting things done is not about how quickly you can go through your to do list, it is about how efficiently you can complete all the tasks at hand. So how do you set the right goals that will help you improve productivity? By making sure that all goals you set fit the SMART criteria.

Specific

Having a specific goal as opposed to having a general one has a much bigger chance of being accomplished. If you don't know how to set specific goals, it's time that you start asking the right questions. The six 'W' questions may seem very elementary, but you can't move on to the next step without taking care of the basics first. These 6 W's are: -

What: What do you need to get done?

Why: Why do you need to get this done?

Where: Where will you get this done?

Who: Who will get this done?

When: When should this be done?

Which: Which task will be done first?

A general goal would probably look something like "finish book" while a specific one would say "write x pages a day for 4 weeks." Having specific goals will not only help you keep your eyes on the prize but will also give you that sense of accomplishment daily. The more specific the goal is, the easier it is to stay on track and work towards meeting it.

Measurable

Aside from being specific about your goals, you should also be able to track your progress. Measuring progress is an important aspect of goal setting because it allows you to see exactly where you are on something that you've set out to do. It gives you an idea on whether you'll be able to reach your goals at a given time or if you're already at the halfway mark.

Take, for example, the specific goal of writing x pages a day for four weeks. There are certain aspects of this goal that make it measurable. The first one is the number of pages that you are meant to write in a day. At the end of each day, you are able to look back and measure whether you have attained the quota that was targeted. If you have met this quota, then you are able to take pride in your ability to meet your goal. If you have not, you then are empowered with information that will help you measure where things may have gone wrong. This in turn will help you come up with a strategy on how to improve them. In addition, you have another measurable goal of four weeks. So at the end of a four week period, you should have been able to meet a certain quota of pages.

Start asking yourself questions like how many, or how much and you'll be more psyched up to keep your head in the game. Tasks can then be broken down into portions that seem attainable.

Attainable

When you specifically identify your goals, you begin to see the road you need to take in order to reach them. This also happens as a result of creating a criteria that is measurable. It's not just about reaching a specific point anymore, you suddenly see the skills, abilities, attitudes, and circumstances you need to develop in order to bring your goals to reality. Once you see the possibility of being able to accomplish something, you begin to plan out your steps wisely.

Also, you should be able to assess whether the goal that you want to meet truly is attainable, because if it is not, you may end up disappointed due to your inability to meet the said goal. An athlete running the 100m sprint may hope to break the world record by achieving a time of 7 seconds for the race. Despite developing their skills through continuous practice and training, they may find that it's hard to move away from the 9 second mark. This does not mean that the athlete is incompetent, it only means that they have set out to accomplish a goal that is not attainable.

When using the SMART technique to set goals, it is imperative that these objectives be attainable and realistic.

Realistic

There's nothing wrong with setting goals that seem too far for you to reach, as long as they're still within the realms of your reality. The runner looking to beat the 100 meter sprint record may have a dream of finishing the race in 7 seconds. However, realistically, they are able to achieve a race in 8 seconds. This will likely still break the existing record, although realistically, it is a target that is more attainable.

Your goals can seem impossible to everyone else, but if they're realistic to you, and you're on the path that will take you to your goal, then that's all that should matter. So if, for example, your goal as to finish law school in 5 years, you'll be able to reach that goal provided that you are enrolled in a law university and raking in the study time. This goes to show that achieving of goals is not automatic, just because you have the intention to achieve them. Certain conditions need to be met in order to consider goals realistic to you.

Timely

Lastly, you goals should have a time frame if you want to be able to reach them. An objective with no time frame doesn't suggest urgency, so you won't be compelled to do anything about it. So if you wanted to lose 20 lbs. for example, your goal shouldn't simply be 'lose 20lbs. someday'. It should be 'lose 20lbs. in 2 months through diet and exercise.' By anchoring your goals on a set time, you work up your mind to begin working towards that objective. Look at the difference between the two goal examples and ask yourself which one would motivate you more? Sometimes, you need that added time pressure to get things done in your life.

When you look at the SMART pattern, it becomes clear that all these aspects are interrelated when you are setting your goals. If you were to follow this criterion with each major goal in your life, you would see a significant difference in how much you can accomplish over s short period of time. The question is, after setting SMART goals, how do you use these goals to increase your productivity? Before anything else, you need to be honest to yourself about the areas that need improvement. I'm sure there are areas in your work ethics and attitude that needs some sprucing up, so this is your time to address that.

Next, identify the factors that are stopping you from reaching your goals. From the lack of sense of urgency or the countless distractions, make sure to list it all down. In addition to your own feelings and behavior towards meeting goals, also consider the factors that may be out of your control that hinder you from achieving your goals. These may include the people around you, your living conditions and so on. Seeing it all on a list will help you understand how you'll be able to move forward with your goals.

Once you've identified the factors that are hindering you from accomplishing your goals, write down the necessary tasks that you need to do for each goal. Break down larger goals into actionable steps and set a reasonable timeline for each. Whereas in research you would create a detailed step by step list, with information about every single task you will be doing at each step, this is not necessary when you are just mapping out your achievable goals. The simpler you're to do list, the more likely you'll be able to go through each task without experiencing any setbacks so try not to over think it.

Lastly, check your progress every week to see if there are any changes. Do an assessment of your action steps to see if any of them proved to be useful to you. Don't forget to keep an eye out for any improvements that you can incorporate into your process.

Chapter 3
Managing your Time to Get Things Done

If you're going to think about it, the term 'time management' is actually a misnomer. You can't manage time per se, you can only manage the events surrounding it. How well you use your time is what's going to determine whether you are successful now and in the future.

For many people, 24 hours in a day just isn't enough. With work, family, and hobbies all demanding time and attention, how do you make sure that you don't waste the limited resource that you have? Even with the best of intentions, many people find themselves wishing that they had done some things differently during the course of the day. The good news is, with careful planning and self control, managing your time is possible. The bad news? It's going to take a lot of work, so you need to be prepared.

People who practice effective time management skills aren't just more productive compared to the people who don't, but they're also less stressed. They are able to complete more tasks, and still have energy to work on their passions at the end of the day. Studies show that people with excellent time management skills also feel better about themselves, allowing them to relate positively with others. This means that there is an all-round improvement in productivity, all because of effective time management.

If you've always wanted to learn the secret to managing time, you need to put together a time management strategy that will best suit your personality, lifestyle, and self discipline. Here are a few strategies on how you can get things done, and use the time to your advantage.

Keep a time log

If you want to manage time, you first need to understand how you use it. Keeping record of how you spend time will help you keep track of your day to day activities, and at the same time, give you better insight on what areas you need to improve. It may seem like a tedious task, but once you get used to it, you'll have a better grasp of your time management skills.

Start by listing down all the activities you do as soon as you're done with each. Include the amount of time that it took you to complete each, and also factor in any distractions or interruptions that may have slowed down the process. Keep in mind the time of day that you were trying to complete a particular task, and where you believe it may be applicable, include this information on your list. After a week, evaluate your results and try to find your pattern. Do you spend too much time commuting to and from the office? Are you guilty of spending hours every day watching TV? Do you waste too much time on social media? Are you more productive in the morning or in the afternoon?

By knowing how you spend your time each day, it will be easier for you to determine a feasible course of action that will help you become better at time management. In this way, getting things done will be a breeze.

Set priorities

Learn how to prioritize so you don't find yourself feeling overwhelmed. Since there's only a certain amount of time in a day, you need to know how to prioritize your tasks, so you know which ones are worth working on. Having priorities will help you keep the right mindset about time management. If you want to really manage your time, you need to understand the distinction between important tasks and urgent tasks. This will help you get things done in the most efficient way possible.

Using your time log, segregate your tasks into 4 categories: urgent, important, not urgent, and not important. Do not leave them in this format, as it may still be a little vague. Add the expected deadlines to each of the tasks so that you know which one to start on first. From there, it will be easier for you to set priorities. In this way, it will become much easier to create and map out a plan of action.

Creating a daily to do list can help you focus on important tasks, regardless of whether they're classified as urgent or not. Just be careful as list making can get a bit overwhelming, especially for those who aren't really that keen on it. Your list should have tasks which are attainable within your time frame of a day. Avoid creating a list that has every little thing that you need to get done, because what happens is at the end of the day, had you not been able to complete all your tasks, you will end up stressed and despondent.

Be Organized

Most people find it hard to manage time when there's that sense of disorganization in your life. Whether it's clutter in your workspace, or in your personal life, you simply can't manage time without managing different aspects of your life. You should start each and every day with a 'clean slate'.

One way to start on organizing is to sort out the clutter in your home and workspace. Categorize your clutter and place them in 3 boxes labeled, "keep", "throw away", and "give away". Once you're done sorting out through all the clutter, make sure to discard your throw away box immediately, and bring your give away box to people who can put it to good use. By dealing with the physical clutter, you'll be mentally and emotionally prepared to manage time better.

When you approach the end of your work day, even though you are exhausted and just want to pack up and leave for home, arrange your work space so that it is ready for you when you come in the following morning. You should have some work trays on your desk where you can place completed tasks, new tasks and those that are still being processed. Leaving a clean desk will make it easier for you to get things done when you go into the office the following day. It will also save you precious time in the morning, as there will be no need for you to start with clean up before you actually get any work done.

Sorting through the clutter basically teaches you how to handle tasks better. Once you've sorted out all information, you can then decide whether to delegate the task to someone else, throw it away or act on it yourself.

Apply Time Boxing

For those who are not familiar with this system, time boxing is when you set a specific time period for your group of tasks. Instead of working a task to completion, time boxing is when you work on a task for a specific amount of time. So if for example, you need to write 3000 words for a blog post you're working on, instead of working on it for x hours until it's done, you'll commit to write as much as you can in 3 hours. It may seem simple, but there's much more to it than meets the eye. The great thing about time boxing is that it allows you to make progress on tasks that seem too daunting or overwhelming. This is because you are able to start at the very least. Once you have started, then the wheels in your head can continue spinning actively, so that should you return to the task, you are actually able to finish it faster and more effectively than if you tried to do it from start to finish in one sitting.

It also puts you ahead of procrastination because the idea if limited time to do something forces you to get started somewhere. You will work harder to complete the task within the allotted time period because you know that after that time, you need to move your concentration and effort to another task.

Stop Multi tasking

If you're one those who think that you save time when you're multi tasking, you're gravely mistaken. Recent studies show that it doesn't put you under pressure when accomplishing tasks, it also causes you to be less productive. Multi tasking forces your brain to focus on different tasks at the same time, which makes it difficult for you to concentrate on specific tasks. In this way, you can never give a task the complete attention that it requires. When this happens, your brain becomes preoccupied with the idea of starting, rather than finishing. If you want to finish tasks and yield better results, it's better to take it one by one.

Although taking tasks one by one may take a little longer time, especially based on the complexity of the task, it is better than trying to multi task and not meeting with any goals.

Chapter 4
Building Habits to Get Things Done

According to Aristotle, "We are what we repeatedly do. Excellence then is not an act, but a habit". We all have our own unique ways of doing things, and starting from childhood, we begin to develop our methods of tackling issues. This is how habits are formed, and there can be good habits or bad habits. In this day and age, a good habit can be quite difficult to build. With distractions readily available wherever you look, developing discipline to get things done can prove to be a challenge. If the success doesn't come overnight, then how are you going to get from point A to point B? Here are a few actionable steps on how to develop strong habits to keep you on the right track.

Be goal oriented

Studies show that being goal oriented is important in building habits that stick. It's that feeling of dreaming big that motivates most people to want to make changes in their life. But as we all know, dreaming big just won't cut it in our day to day routine. It's the daily toil that results in changes. Therefore you need to figure out how you can turn your dreams into reality, and action often does that. Each step that you take should get you closer and closer to some predetermined goal, so that you are conscious of when you are close to achieving your dreams. The challenge to this though is staying motivated for the long haul so that you are able to build the right habits.

So how do you stay motivated to build habits? By setting macro goals for yourself to establish what you want to achieve in the long run then set little micro goals as well that will help make the macro goals measurable. Take the quota approach and establish the minimum amount of work you need to do every day before you can consider yourself a success. This makes the long term goal much more approachable and doable. So next time you're losing a bit of motivation, focus on the day to day goals instead of directing full focus on your big picture goals. Think of these micro goals as stepping stones that will lead you to the attaining your macro goal because without them, you won't really have anything to step on.

Develop triggers

Another way to make sure that habits stick is by developing triggers for them. Triggers are often associated with negative behavior, for example, one may feel triggered to smoke just before they have a meal. This trigger becomes a part of their daily routine, thus forming a habit. However, one can use triggers positively to get things done, by simply attaching some additional behavior to what is already being done on a daily basis.

Don't try to change your routine off the bat. Find ways to incorporate new habits into the routine you already have. So instead of aiming to write 1000 words per day at a specific interval, aim to incorporate this into your current routine. Write 500 words after brushing your teeth in the morning and another 500 at night before you start getting ready to go to bed. By picking out a regular activity in your schedule and using that as a trigger to forge new habits, it will be easier for you to include it in your new routine. Before you know it, you will automatically be able to write out 500 words twice a day. It's like adding a link to an already existing chain. The stronger your trigger, the better the chances are that the new habit will stick. Don't just rely on sheer willpower to build better habits. Some basic planning can go a long way.

Simplify your routine

If you find your current lifestyle to be quite overwhelming, chances are you won't find it easy to build new habits. This often happens if you have a very long to do list, where everything seems to be urgent, and you are trying your best to meet more goals that you are able to in the limited time of a day.

According to experts, it's easier to make habits stick when you're dealing with a simple routine. This means that you create a schedule that is attainable, where you can start and finish one task at a time, and thereby fully utilize all the time you have in a day. Having too many decisions doesn't just make you lose focus on what you want to achieve, but it also makes it harder for you to get used to new habits. This is because you are constantly catching up, worrying about the next task, being preoccupied and generally, never really getting anything done.

Thinking of every day concerns, no matter how mundane or pleasant, can deplete your mental energy and affect how your brain copes with developing new habits. If you want to develop long term discipline, take your busy routine down a notch and start making fewer decisions. Take on fewer tasks in the day, and allow yourself the freedom to work smart rather than working too hard.

Stop fantasizing about end results

One mistake that many people make when trying to build new habits is that they lose sight of the reasons why they want to make the change. It's easy to get caught up with the end result that many people forget about the small details. This is perhaps there is an underlying message out there that people need to visualize what they hope to achieve. This message is positive if taken in the correct context and applied correctly.

There's nothing wrong with visualizing the goals you want to reach, but if you visualize it too much without visualizing the work required, you're only setting yourself up for disappointment. Simply put, those who visualize the process of work in order to achieve the end result are far more likely to stick to the new habits compared to those who choose to visualize the end result alone. This ties in with setting your macro goals and micro goals to reach your goal. Visualizing the process doesn't just direct attention to the steps needed to reach the goal and it can also reduce a level of anxiety as you are able to see what needs to be done to get to your desired goals. It makes achieving success through getting things done measurable.

Change your perspective

Since new habits are often considered to be very fragile, it's important that you also learn to change your perspective towards the process. Eliminate all negative thoughts that might lead you to not follow through on what you're trying to develop. These are the negative thoughts that creep in when you face some difficulties establishing your new habits. They lead you to doubt your abilities, or the point that you are trying to improve upon or change. Expect that there are times when you will rather give up, but know that it's just part of the process. In fact, when you face these challenges you can rest assured that you are doing something that is working. The thing with change is that it is never comfortable and pleasant, but it does pay off significantly, in the long run.

So how do you avoid abandoning ship when things start to get tough? By examining the habit and looking at the areas that need improving on. If for example you're having a hard time waking up early in the mornings, try to pinpoint the reasons why. Is it because you are sleeping too late in the evenings? Are you thinking constantly before bed so it takes forever for your mind to switch off? Might it be dietary? There are so many reasons that you may have an issue with breaking a habit. Once you see what exactly is stopping the habit from sticking, create an action plan to eliminate whatever the culprit is. Don't give into the frustration when habits aren't working out the way you expected. Just go back to the beginning and change your perspective.

Chapter 5
Putting an End to Procrastination to Get Things Done

When you are doing a task that you enjoy, you can hardly wait to get into it, start it and follow through all the way to the end. Attaining that result makes you particularly satisfied, and it also helps that you enjoy the entire process of doing so. However, if you are working on a task that you do not enjoy, that seems harder than most, is time consuming or generally boring, you will not have the same motivation as if you loved what you were doing. At this point, you will put it off for as long as you possibly can, meaning that you procrastinate.

We all have that tendency to procrastinate. From the smallest things like sorting out files to the more complex tasks like finding a new job, procrastination can really put a dent on your capacity to achieve more. And it doesn't just hurt your productivity overall, but it also lead you to emotional turmoil. Procrastination robs you the joy of finally reaching those long held aspirations. This is because you end up in a state of anxiety and worry because of the tasks that you have been unable to complete.

There are all sorts of creative reasons for not being able to do things you want to do now. Whether it's because you're too busy, too broke, too stressed, or too inexperienced, valid as these reasons may be from your standpoint, you can't ignore the fact these reasons are stopping you from reaching for those goals. Whatever your reason may be bounded on, it's stopping you from putting in real work to reach your goals. The deeper you look into these reasons you will find that they center on excuses. You *can* complete a particular task should you choose to, you are just not motivated to do so.

So how do you put an end to procrastination and finally start on getting things done? Before you can put an end to procrastination, you first need to address the real issue that is stopping you from moving. And more often than not, it's the emotion of fear that hinders growth. Fear in its deepest sense was designed to alert our minds and protect us from experiencing pain. While it urges us away from anything that could rattle our world and injure our pride, fear left unchecked can also render us stagnant. Fear fuels us with reasons to not take chances. We tell ourselves that we'll make our move when the right time comes, but the right time never comes. Instead, we're left to our own devices, making more excuses to justify why we're not getting anything done.

The most effective way to put an end to procrastination is by believing that life rewards those who take action. You need to have faith that what you are doing is being done well, to the best of your ability. Whether the result is what you expected or does not meet expectations, you should rest assured that you put your best foot forward and tried to attain the best result that you could. You can't accomplish anything if you'll sit still and wait for circumstances to get better. If you're ready to free yourself from procrastination, here are some ways on how you can take bold action to improve your life and get things done.

Set your Goals

Without goals, you won't have any reason to move. This is why goal setting isn't just an activity that you can overlook. It should give you direction and motivation to achieve whatever you set your mind to. While you are setting your goals, add an element of time to them. This will stop you from pushing them forward over and over again. For example, you may need to write a report for work, which you have been pushing forward for ages. You can set a goal to complete the first chapter in two days, that way, in two days you are able to look back and see whether you have attained your goal.

Use the earlier chapter on how to set goals to guide you. If you feel intimidated by your goals, try breaking it into steps to make it more manageable. You don't have to memorize every single step. You just need to know the next few steps to get you moving forward. The next steps will just come naturally as you go along.

Harness the power of visualization

The power of visualization can do wonders, especially if when you start slipping back into procrastination. There are certain emotions that are associated with success, and these include relief, joy, peace, and satisfaction. Imagining the emotional high that you'll feel when you finally finish a task should be enough to motivate you to take that first step. It is important that you do not overwhelm yourself with all the details that the task requires, all you need to do is just take the first step. Picture yourself celebrating the fruits of your labor. You may not be able to celebrate soon, but knowing that you're getting closer and closer as the days go by is a great way to keep excited about your tasks. Find the time to celebrate the little things as you move forward so that you have something to fuel that excitement whenever you visualize.

Face your fears

Fear can have tremendous power over your life, that's if you let it. You may not even realize that you are fearful until you take the time to truly evaluate why you are procrastinating on particular tasks. One way to combat the fear of failing is to focus on what you want to achieve and not on the things you don't want to happen. Do not think about missing the deadline, getting the details wrong, disappointing your boss or anything else that may settle in your mind and cause you stress.

If you let fear continue to disable you, the years will pass you by so fast and one day you'll wake up with nothing to show for them. The only way to really get moving is to be honest with yourself and address the thoughts that keep you from taking that first step. Whenever you feel like you're procrastinating, take time to deal with the fear that you don't want to address.

Have accountability

Being responsible for your actions empowers you to change them when necessary. With the responsibility comes accountability, whereby should you have to explain your actions, you are able to do so, and own your actions and decisions.

You can also fight procrastination with the help of a support system or accountability partner. Having a team to back you up whenever you start to feel defeated can help you stay on the right track. Whenever things get tough, it helps to have a sounding board to help process your frustration. Thereby it is important that you find someone who can offer you this support, and you in turn should support them, in the same way.

Reward yourself

Don't forget to reward yourself whenever you pass through the milestones of your journey. Rewards can be small things that you give yourself, or could even be a simple pat on your back, and they hold an enormous amount of emotional motivation. Whether it's a fun thing to do with friends or some alone time, rewarding progress and effort makes it easier to undo procrastination. You need to reinforce the feeling of accomplishment with positive rewards so that you won't be tempted to go back to your old habits.

Chapter 6
Creating a Plan to Get Things Done

In the previous chapters, it has been mentioned that you need to be able to set goals so that you can get things done, and these include both macro goals and micro goals. Once you have set these goals, you still need to take one more step, and that is to create a plan of action.

A plan will outline the steps that you are going to take, and will help you on a day to day basis to assess whether you are actually meeting your goals. A plan adds an element of deeper detail than you would find with outlined goals.

So how really does a plan help you get things done? Think of it as a blueprint.

Components of your Plan

Many people find planning quite daunting and may choose not to because they lack understanding about how effectively a plan can change your working situation. It is always good to have a plan that is as detailed as possible, but even though you take just five minutes to draft out a plan, it can make a major difference to whether or not you are able to get things done. To start creating your plan, you need to have an idea of what you are looking to accomplish, and the best way is to start from your desired end goal and work your way backward. Therefore to begin, list out all of your macro goals. Your macro goals should be SMART goals so that you are able to check and assess whether you are meeting them.

The next step is to list out the micro goals for each of the macro goals. This breaks down the process more and gives an idea of the path that you intend to follow to attain your goals.

For example, a marketer could set a macro goal of selling 10,000 units of their product by the end of the year. Then, they move on to their micro goals, which could be to sell a certain number of units in each month. With these types of goals, it makes it easier to assess issues along the way, and, of course, to resolve them.

Once you have listed your micro goals, you can then list out the tasks that need to be completed to meet your micro goals. This is where the deeper element of planning begins to take root. So, going back to the example, at the micro level the marketer intends to sell a certain number of units in each month. When evaluating the tasks, the marketer may detail who the target market is, how they will be reached and any activities that will be executed to complete the sales. At this stage, it makes it easier to understand how that macro goal will be achieved, and the reality that it can be achieved becomes much clearer.

Tying up the Loop Holes

Now that you have put together the components of your plan it is time to get organized and tie up all the loop holes. Loop holes are those parts of the plan that have not been fully explained or addressed. If they are not dealt with adequately at the planning stage, they could cause major issues in the future which may mean that you do not get anything done.

These loop holes include information on budgeting, advertising, team work and so on. They are aspects of the plan that need to be in place so that the plan is executed.

Develop a Checklist

There is one way that you can keep tabs on whether you are following through with your plan on a daily basis, and that is be creating a check list. A check list basically has everything you need to accomplish for the day listed out, with a space on the side to tick the task once it is completed. It helps you keep track of what you have managed to complete for the day, and can be an indication of whether you have tried to cram too much into a short period of time.

When planning to get things done for the day, you may have a major task that you need to complete. A checklist allows you to break down this large tasks into manageable parts so that you can keep tabs on minor goals.

A checklist allows you to see whether you have too much to do in one day, thereby helping you make the decision to delegate some tasks so that they overall work can be done by the stipulated deadline. You are also able to review your activities and identify any time wasting or low value tasks that will deter you from the overall goal without providing any special benefits. These items can be relegated to the bottom of your list, meaning that you are able to get the most important things done within an acceptable time frame.

Prioritize

Once you start to create a plan, you will be able to prioritize. This means that you are able to evaluate which tasks are more important than others, helping you decide what you should start or finish with, and how this will impact your overall plan of action.

Prioritizing helps you to take note of the deadline, and complete the most important tasks before you reach that deadline. This ensures that you always get the job done, and even if for whatever reason you run out of time, the task that is central to the functioning of what was needed is adequately completed.

Know your Motivations

Ask yourself a question, why are you creating a plan in the first place? What is the desired end results and why do you hope to attain it? To get things done, you need to have some positive motivations to drive you forward. Often people work with fear as their basis, and what happens is that they find themselves unable to be productive. If you are doing something so that you do not lose your job, you will be worried about losing your job, and, therefore, may not give that task the full attention that it needs. However, if you are doing a task because you want a promotion, your approach will be entirely different, and you will surely give it your very best effort.

Chapter 7
Living in the Present to Get Things Done

From an early age, many people are taught to plan for their future. As a child, you may have been encouraged to save so that you could buy a toy you like. Or you could have waited for a special day that you had planned for, like a birthday party. It is an excellent idea to plan for the future but it does have its drawbacks, and that is that you miss the present moment.

Take for example you are planning a birthday party. You know that in order for the party to be a success, you must get every little detail right. So you spend a substantial amount of time putting things together in the hope that it will be a success. By the time the date of the party comes, you are exhausted from all the planning, and probably just want to get it over and done with. However, you are still anxious and anticipating what it will be like. If you do not get the turnout or success that you were expecting, you will be sorely disappointed, and discouraged for the future. The sad thing is in all that process, you missed out on the present and only focused on the future event.

There is another scenario whereby one does not live in the present, and that is living in the past. Rather than working on achieving new goals in life, you spend your time reminiscing about when you had a great success. You try and relive it over and over again in the hope that you will experience the same results. So instead of trying out new things, you repeatedly go through the motions that you took in the past. However, the more you try to repeat what happened, the less you actually achieve, which just like living in the future, may lead to disappointment and discouragement. It is not possible to relive a moment in the exact same way it previously occurred.

Instead one can choose to use the joyful experience to create a base for a new opportunity.

When a person is disappointed and discouraged, they will lack motivation and will be unable to get anything done. It is at these moments that they are their weakest, and also their most vulnerable. The solution to getting things done is to live in the present.

How to Be Present

In the previous chapter, creating a plan has been discussed, and within that, a method of keeping track of your daily activities to see whether you meet your predetermined milestones. Living in the present is all about *how* you carry out those activities that you need to meet on a day to day basis. It all starts with your plan.

The key to getting things done, and getting them done well, is to respect every step of the process. So just as much as you are working towards achieving your macro goal, you need to put a substantial amount of energy in executing your micro goals, and your daily tasks. Living in the present entails giving the daily tasks the full concentration that they deserve, so that at the end of the day, you have given 100% of your self to everything that you approach – even the activities that you do not find enjoyable.

As you teach yourself to be present and complete things at the moment, you can ask yourself one question, and that is, how would I complete this task if there was no tomorrow? You will begin to realize that when you see something as your last chance or opportunity to make good, then your entire attitude will shift.

You will begin to focus on what you are doing, in such a way that you can appreciate your mood, thoughts, and disposition as you are doing the task. When your general awareness of self increases, so does your motivation to do the right thing, and savor the present.

When you are living in the present, you will want to enjoy each moment, and, therefore, you will reduce all the activities that may dull your awareness to the moment. In this way, you will be able to get more done as you would avoid idle chatter, day dreaming, zoning out of conversations or simply having a passive state of mind.

Take Action

Living in the present calls you to be action oriented in order to get things done. You will be motivated to avoid distractions, and work hard to attain goals. One thing that stops people from taking action is conceptualizing. A concept is something that you would like to achieve following some type of guidelines, but in actuality, it does not exist. It is simply an idea.

When most people come up with an idea. They can visualize it coming to pass. They then focus on the idea to the extent that everything else around them suffers. A concept is something that has not yet come into existence, and focusing on it will stop you from taking action, because you are waiting for some future eventuality.

Practice Mindfulness

Mindfulness is a state of being conscious or having awareness of a situation. It entails focusing on the present moment while also acknowledging and accepting your thoughts, feelings, and bodily sensations. Living in the present to get things down requires you to differentiate between your present thoughts and your future thoughts. Whether you like it or not, your mind will always have thoughts passing through it. To live in the present and get things done, you need to be able to hear all these thoughts, and then pick and choose the ones that will be beneficial for you in the present moment. It is, therefore, pointless to try and stop your mind from generating thoughts.

Mindfulness encourages you to be more aware of your actions and focus on what you are doing. When you are focused, your mind is less likely to distract itself by thinking a myriad of other thoughts, or giving itself up to other topics. Mindfulness encourages you to live in the moment, and in doing so, you will make sure to get the most out of it.

Chapter 8
Establishing Rewards to Get Things Done

In pre-school, when a little boy or girl does well in class or at an activity, they are given a reward. Often, this reward would be a star in their report book, or even a special badge that they get to wear for the entire day. When they wear a badge, everyone knows that they have done something exceptional, and they are able to experience pride in their accomplishments. This then motivates them to accomplish more in everything that they do.

As adults, we are still the same in regards to our mentality towards rewards. Rewards serve as a motivation to get things done. Take for example you work in a busy organization and directly serve customers. At the entrance of your office, there is a framed picture of the employee of the month. Every single person that walks in sees the face of this lucky employee and is delighted if they find that they are being served by the best. That employee will have a sense of pride, and likely increase their productivity so that they can retain the title. For all the others around, they will work harder to have that coveted spot.

Rewards, however are not just about receiving recognition that can be seen and acknowledged by other people. You can establish rewards for yourself to encourage you to meet a goal. This is often seen in people who are trying to diet in order to lose weight. They are likely to reward themselves with a 'treat' if they meet a particular goal or go through a period with limited foods. It is simple to establish rewards, but how can you get started?

Select your Milestones

When establishing rewards, you must select your milestones carefully. Milestones are points on a journey where you meet a particular goal or complete the task. As you meet your milestone, you are then able to go on to the next level or the coming task. At each milestone, you can give yourself a reward.

Take, for example, you have an eight hour work day. You create a checklist of tasks that you need to complete within each hour. Should you complete your task before the time is up you can give yourself a reward of a snack, a break, or some personal surfing of the internet.

Although this may seem to be a small action when working towards attaining a goal, it can be incredibly successful as a motivation tool. If you have something enjoyable to look to for a job well done, you are highly likely going to do the best you can at the task at hand. This is because you then avoid needing to report the said task, and you can enjoy a reward that is highly personal to suit your individual needs.

Build on your Rewards

Sometimes when someone thinks of a reward, they imagine a massive prize that is given to a winner on a podium with a crowd cheering on. However, this is not the case. Rewards can be small and personal, in just the same way that they can be large and ostentatious. Start off with allowing yourself small rewards for completing day to day tasks. As you go along, you should build on your rewards so that by the time you get to your macro goal, you receive a sizeable reward.

This can be particularly helpful when you are looking to getting work done. Say for example you would like to begin a reward scheme at your workplace. For purposes of this example, it is assumed you are a marketer. You may request for a commission reward should you reach a specified sales quota within a month. Then, if you surpass your targets for six months consecutively, you should negotiate for a substantial pay rise. This would be a micro goal. As a macro goal, you may negotiate for a bigger reward if you triple your revenue within a year. The reward would need to be substantial, for example, a brand new car.

The great thing about having rewards like these at different levels, is that once you attain one, you are more motivated to work towards the next stage until you get to the ultimate reward. Therefore, you will ensure that you complete the tasks that you need to in order to earn this reward.

Reward your Team

The earlier part of this section was focused on how you can experience rewards for your own effort. If you are in a management position within an organization, to get things done, you may need substantial input from people who work below you. In that instance, it becomes even more imperative to establish and implement a reward scheme.

In order to reward your team successfully, you need to determine what motivates them to get things done. There are basically two types of motivation, and they are intrinsic or extrinsic motivation. Someone who has intrinsic motivation prefers to be rewarded in a way that elevates their pride in the workplace, whereas someone with extrinsic motivation would prefer to be rewarded financially. Understanding what works for your team will help to increase their incentive to work, which should lead to improved productivity.

Rewards in this sense do not need to be purely financial. They may include getting an additional day off every month due to hard work, increase in the benefits that are earned as part of the monthly remuneration or even new equipment at the work place, such as a lap top. The way to making rewarding your team successful lies in being able to identify what their needs are. Once that has been established, the staff will be more motivated to improve on their work because they would be able to see the benefits.

There is not denying that a good work environment that appreciates the workforce with praise, money, tangible goods and other rewards will be more productive than an environment where there is limited recognition and no incentives to work. Establishing rewards is effective in getting things done, whether you establish the rules on your own for your personal motivation, or whether your organization creates incentives to motivate you to work harder.

Chapter 9
Seeing the Bigger Picture to Get Things Done

Before you tackle a task, you need to know how it fits into the grand scheme of things. When you are able to see the bigger picture, you are better equipped to create a detailed plan, as well as to follow through as intended.

Take for example, an organization is looking to launch a new product. They want to reach an audience of 3,000 people on the launch night. Here, their bigger picture is that once they reach 3,000 people, this will translate into sales that will increase their bottom line. Therefore, everything that needs to happen with the launch should bear in mind that the bottom line is to reach 3,000 people, and make them customers.

The person who is planning to get things done is then expected to look beyond the launch night, at the possibility of establishing a long term relationship with the customer. This thinking will affect the nature of the advertising program and design of the launch event, and even the method in which the attendees are contacted.

When working towards getting things done, there is a difference between just meeting the expected goals and finishing the tasks, and finishing the tasks very well in an attempt to cross them off a checklist. If one is focused on seeing the bigger picture, when they are working towards meeting their goal, they will ensure that they utilize the very best of their skills and resources.

Being a Successful Leader

When getting things done in the workplace, a primary leadership quality is the ability to see the bigger picture. This requires that the leader has a deep understanding of all the macro goals for the firm.

Seeing the picture also entails a certain personality trait, and that is maintaining a positive attitude. Positivity can lead to the accomplishment of goals much faster, and much easier than a mindset of negativity would allow.

To really be successful at getting things done, a successful leader should be able to get the entire team to also see the bigger picture. Once they do so, there will be a shared vision, and everyone will become clearer as to the role they are expected to fulfill.

Tips for Seeing the Bigger Picture

These tips will work wonders in helping you to see the bigger picture. They are: -

• **View the entire task** – In earlier chapters, creating a plan was discussed. This is where this point comes in and finds relevance. When you are working towards something, even on a daily basis supporting mundane activities, it is vital that you view the entire task from beginning to end, rather than simple seeing only the parts.

• **Understand why you are working** – When a person is working blindly without any reflection on what the firm would like to achieve, then that person is more likely to simply go through the motions when they are at the work place, than to really take time to know what they are doing. One must know what they are doing, how they will do it and why they are doing it.

• **Visualize your Destination** – Take time to paint pictures in your mind of what the end game is meant to be.

Visualizing is perhaps the easiest way to see the bigger picture, as visualizing requires one to think beyond what is right in front of them, and focus on bigger and better things.

- **Achievements and Teams** – When you are working towards meeting a future target, you will usually need to incorporate other people to help you meet the goals. Therefore, you should make room for teams within your vision. With teams, comes little achievements that you will make along the way. There should be measurable, and rewarded with each passing step.

Taking a Step Back

When you are working towards meeting a macro goal, on a day to day basis, you will probably focus on dealing with all the little details and actions steps required to move from one point to another. You would be ticking items on your checklist, trying to this as efficiently as possible, and making sure that you meet all your won stipulated milestones. All this is what you have been aiming to do, and, in a nutshell, it is good to keep yourself on track each day. However, there are times when you need to stop, take a step back and assess what you are actually doing.

The reason is, you may end up so caught up in all the little details and steps that you are accomplishing on a day to day basis that you lose sight of the bigger picture which will help you to get things done more efficiently and possibly even faster than expected. You will realize this when not matter how much effort you put in on a daily basis, you do not seem to be moving ahead as you thought you would, and each day and week becomes the same. The result is that your work becomes tedious instead of being fulfilling.

When you take a step back to view the bigger picture, you will be able to pick out any flaws more easily. Perhaps there is something that needs to be changed to the processes that you are using, or you have delegated tasks to someone who is ineffective. You might even need to go back to the drawing board and completely redefine your plan. It is better to do this as you go along, than to risk being stuck in a particular position for a long period of time.

Taking a step back also helps to bring the final goal into focus. This way, you are able to assess whether you are still on track or how far down you have gone down the wrong path. You may be doing all the right things, but the circumstances around you that are completely out of your control have changed. These include the other people who you may have depended on to bring your goal to fruition, the economic environment and so on. This requires you to go back to the drawing board and chart a new course in order to get things done.

Chapter 10
Shutting out the Noise to Get Things Done

The moment you start to pursue a project, you are likely to be hit with a range of obstacles all working towards hindering your movements towards your goal. It is those obstacles that are hereby referred to as noise.

Traditionally, when one thinks of noise, they may consider loud sounds like booming music, aero planes and the like. However, noise is so much more than that. Noise can include visual distraction, information clutter, loud sounds, misdirected individuals – in fact, anything that will distract you from your chosen path to accomplish tasks may be categorized as noise.

Visual Distractions

Picture that you have designed your plan and have done so meticulously. You may have even created a chart where you have managed to lay out all your ideas using illustrations such as graphs, charts and target diagrams. You are expecting to use this chart to make it easier to accomplish your day to day activities. However, every time that you look at the chart, you notice a detail or two that is missing, and you feel that you need to cover all your bases in order for your plan to work. So then you formulate a way that you can fill in this loop hole to ensure that you have a sound plan. The more you look, the more loop holes you find, and before you know it, you are trying desperately to fill in all the loop holes in your plan, but you have not actively started to bring your plan to life.

The visual representation of what you are hoping to accomplish has proven to be a major distraction. As much as you need to get your plan perfect, you must remember that your plan is just an outline, and it needs to be flexible one at that. This is because inevitably, as you go along with its execution, you will have to make some changes to deal with your existing environment. Getting stuck at the planning phase means that you will never get things done.

Information Clutter

In promotions, executives will talk about information clutter and how it affects a consumer. Information clutter is basically all the advertisements that a consumer is bombarded with to the extent that the consumer becomes numb to the messages because they are too many to process. This overflow of information can also affect how we get things done.

A simple example to illustrate this is to consider what it takes to write a report for the workplace. You are asked to submit a report on your ideas for seeing the bigger picture and time management, and the report should include four unique points that can be applied to your work environment. You decide to do your research on the internet, and when you type in your words to the search engine, you are informed that there are over 3 million results that fit into your keywords. The challenge for you is choosing the sites that are most relevant so that you can pick your information from there.

If you are an extreme perfectionist, you may be inclined to review all the information that is available so that you can select the most viable points, but with 3 million pages to read through, you would never complete the report. This excess of information can form an element of noise when you are looking to get things done.

This noise will overwhelm you, and lead you to give up on your task as you may doubt your ability to overcome all the issues to meet your goals. Deciphering the noise, and choosing the most helpful information according to your ability will make it easier for you to navigate towards your goals.

Distracting Colleagues

As no man is an island, one must always consider how they will work with other people in order to get things done. Other people become a form of noise when they cannot see your vision, and thereby attempt to distract you from your plan, or even change your plan altogether. They can do this in various ways.

The first way would be through discouraging you. There are people who seem to be eternally pessimistic when it comes to their outlook on things. They are always looking for the problems in a plan, or all the things that could go wrong. Although a little pessimism and criticism can be useful, too much of this will be counterproductive. The result is that you will find yourself deviating from your plan, because the belief that it could work would be stripped away from you. In that regard, you would not get anything done.

The other way that people could be distracting is in their inability to complete the delegated tasks. The reason this becomes a form of noise is because it greatly interrupts the ability of the team to meet the desired goals. What happens in this instance is that other members of the team are forced to pick up the slack from the dormant member, and, in this case, they cannot get their tasks done effectively. The result is that nothing gets done properly, and the quality of the work suffers greatly.

Finally, people can be a form of noise when their motivation does not match with your motivation. What happens is that you are heading towards the same goal, though you ae using two completely different path ways to get there. This will lead to some friction, as both sides will be sure that their way is better, and time will be wasted on justifications and defense mechanisms on how the work is being done. This will slow down the work being done, as everyone will be too busy trying to be right, and then attempting to meet the goals.

Noise is more than a temporary distraction or set back. It can have detrimental effects on a plan. Therefore, it should be recognized as early as possible, and dealt with before it becomes a major distraction that deviates the entire plan. Noise has the ability of ensuring that nothing gets done, and everyone is permanently distracted. When planning, simple suggestions should be put in place to deal with noise.

Chapter 11
Avoiding Interruptions to Get Things Done

It would be so amazing if it was possible to execute a plan from beginning to end without having to worry about interruptions. This, unfortunately, is not a realistic way to view planning because inevitably, things will happen along the way that throw a spanner in the works.

There are so many ways that a plan can get interrupted so that it becomes difficult to get things done. These ways include: -

- Lack of resources

- Changes in the external environment

- Changes in the internal environment

- Disappointing team members

- Overflow of work

- Emergency urgent tasks

- Lack of time

When you face these and other interruptions, what suffers most is your work. The reason is that these interruptions cause you to feel a lack of control, and, therefore, you are unable to get anything done. Your grasp of organization and planning will take a hit, and you will feel as though you are picking up pieces constantly instead of putting together the entire puzzle. This chapter shall take a brief look at each of these interruptions and suggest how they can be avoided.

Lack of Resources

Once you decide to carry out a plan or a task, it would be ideal to start and finish it with ease. However, once you begin, you may discover that you are unable to complete the plan because you have run out of resources. This interruption can easily be averted at the planning stage. Before any plan is approved for execution, it is important to review it from all angles and ensure that there are enough resources available to complete the plan. If the resources are limited at the beginning of the execution, a guaranteed source of resources mid plan should be anticipated.

When a person is starting a project that is funded by another party, they may begin working on the project hoping that if they meet their milestones, they will continue to get funding. When they fail to meet these milestones, they discover that they are unable to meet their goals as the resources dry up. This will mean that nothing in the end gets done, and time and resources have been wasted unnecessarily. To avoid this, one should remember that planning is key.

Changes in the External Environment

There is a whole range of situational factors that are out of a person's control, and these mainly have to do with the external environment. When looking to get things done, there are some interruptions that you cannot overcome on your own. These include political upheavals, freak weather patterns, national strikes and so on. A plan may come to a complete halt because of them.

There is something that can be done to avoid these interruptions, and that is looking at the past when creating a plan. The best predictor of future behavior is past behavior, so if you are able to identify a pattern in the past behavior, you will be able to consider that pattern for future happenings.

These situational factors can be incorporated into your long term plan as 'just in case' scenarios, whereby you have a plan b and plan c of how you will continue towards your goal incase these changes actually happen and affect the way you are doing things.

Changes in the Internal Environment

These changes refer to things that happen within your immediate environment, or factors that may affect you directly. There could be changes in your lifestyle such as a change of location due to moving house, a new addition to your family or a restructuring of the organization that you are working with. Although these changes can happen suddenly, they do not happen overnight. Therefore, there is always time to evaluate what you are trying to get done, and come up with ways to complete the task without having to stop things meaning that nothing gets done.

Sometimes, changes in the internal environment can lead to a temporary period of suspension or pause of a plan though, with the appropriate options in place, this may be avoided completely.

Disappointing Team Members

The thing about working in teams is that everyone is meant to execute a particular task so that the overall picture comes together nicely. We are not all the same though, so whenever one works in a team setting, there should be some psychological preparation for that team member who will not pull their weight. These people are the ones who can bring an entire project to a halt, due to their inability to complete their tasks and quite possibly, to take responsibility for their actions.

To avoid this type of interruption so that you can get things done, you should do a serious assessment of each and every team member before they become a part of your team. If the end goal is important to you, do not use your platform as an opportunity to give people second chances, or to allow them to do what they can to bring your plan to fruition. Choose a team of experienced and competent people, who will ensure that you are able to keep to your stipulated timeline, by being results oriented and focused on efficiency.

Overflow of Work

Too much of a good thing is a bad thing. Whether it is too many people to see in a day, too many emails to respond to, too many actions to take or an overflowing to do list, having more work than you can manage will interrupt your ability to get things done. When one is overwhelmed, they become worried, and this can have drastic effects on their focus. This interruption can be avoided by creating and putting some systems in place.

For example, in a busy office, one can have a limit to the number of people they can see in a day so that they have time to finish off any pending tasks they may face. Having a grip on one's schedule also becomes very important. Over time, you will notice that your day follows a particular pattern, and you can expect a certain amount of work. Therefore, scheduling can make it easier to get things done. Rather than replying each and every email when it comes in, you may choose to set aside time during the day just to reply emails, for example for an hour in the morning, and an hour in the afternoon. This means that you will not spend your entire day answering emails to the detriment of your other work.

You should also have some sort of structure set up for your day. There are tasks that should be executed at quiet times, such as upgrading systems and maintenance, so as to avoid having to stop work leading to things not getting done.

Emergency Urgent Tasks

These can really get your work, of course, especially if you have already created a plan and are trying to meet a certain target for the day. These emergency tasks are usually things that need to be done with great urgency, so that someone else within the organization is able to meet their targets for the day. If you have planned yourself well, you will not have any of these of your own, and you should be able to get things done efficiently.

The best way to deal with these is to be straightforward with your co-workers about your ability to fit emergency tasks into your plan. If you are dealing with your boss, it may feel a little uncomfortable to inform them that they are interrupting your work flow. You should still communicate with them about this though so that they can then make the decision to continue with the interruption or to respect your work ethic. To also keep the peace with your team, you can have some time allocated within your week solely for dealing with emergency tasks that arise.

Lack of Time

The best laid plans all face one issue, and that is the lack of time. People are so busy each day that often times they may wish that a day had more than 24 hours so that they could get everything done. If you are working with a checklist or plan, then you would have exercised some time management as you are planning your tasks. The issue comes in when a task takes longer than expected, which affects everything else and leads to things not getting done.

To deal with this interruption, you should avoid packing your day too tightly. You can allow for some time after each task, just in case and extra fifteen minutes is needed. This will ensure that you are not constantly under pressure, meaning that you will be better equipped to handle a situation should things not go according to plan.

Chapter 12
Using all the Hours in a Day to Get Things Done

Each day you are presented with one thousand, four hundred and forty minutes (24 hours) to get things done. This is something that you can count on without fail, that you will have 24 hours in each day. Time management is challenging, and utilizing the entire day effectively may seem impossible. There are ways that you can achieve efficient time management, and these ways are outlined in this chapter.

To start, you should go through three or four days and keep a log or a journal with information on what you did through the day. This will help you assess how much time you spend on working, eating, commuting, sleeping and extra activities. Once you create a log, you may be surprised to find out what you have been doing with your time. Getting things done calls for effective time management.

The activities that you are likely to encounter are as follows: -

Sleep

This is perhaps one of the most underestimated methods of getting things done that has been exposed. Many people often view the time they sleep as extra time in a day to get things done. 'Workaholics' will often carry their work home so that they can sleep less and get more work done. However, sleep is vital when you want to get things done.

A good night's sleep will positively affect your concentration and your general wellbeing. One should aim to get a minimum of 6 hours sleep in a night. The ideal amount of sleep is 8 hours a night, and at the very most 10 hours a night. Sleep allows the body to rest and rejuvenate, and people who get enough sleep are better able to function due to increased energy levels.

Getting Ready

Whether you are preparing to go to work or attend a function, a certain amount of time can be allocated to getting ready in a day. A good time allocation for getting ready is one hour. If one is getting ready in the morning, they can use that one hour to wake up, have a shower and brush their teeth, have something to eat for breakfast, and then head out to start their day. Anything more than an hour to complete this timing is excessive and means that you are not managing your time well. Although time spent on personal grooming can be relative, within an hour, one should be able to get most of their personal grooming done.

Commuting

If you work away from home, this time needs to be factored into your day. The time you spend commuting depends entirely on your distance away from your workplace. Most people find ways to save time while commuting so that they can get things done. To manage this time, you may choose to commute during off peak hours rather than during peak or rush hours. In addition, using public transportation like the train, may be more effective than using your private car.

Working

Based on your job description and contract, you will be expected to work for a certain number of hours each day. When time management is discussed, it is often the hours that you spend at work that come under the most scrutiny. It is during this period that you would have created a checklist of all the things that you need to do, and where you would working down your checklist and assessing your progress at the end of the day.

Normally, eight hours in a day are allocated for work, and within these eight hours, one needs to get a lot of things done.

Eating and Sustenance

The average person will consume five meals a day. These are three main meals being breakfast, lunch and dinner, and two snacks in the mid morning and midafternoon. The time it takes to eat is normally minimal, although a large amount of time is wasted at meal times.

The time to consume breakfast is incorporated into the getting ready time in the morning. Lunch is often allocated one hour in the day, which is the same with dinner. Snacks are often allocated half an hour each. With this basic information, the amount of time that should be allocated to meals is three hours of each day.

Exercise

Just as sleep is important for the body to function at its peak, so is exercise. A certain amount of time needs to be allocated for exercise every day, to keep the body fit and maintain overall health. This will go a long way in helping ensure that things do get done.

The minimum amount of time spent on exercise each day should be around thirty minutes. Ideally an hour of exercise each day is the preferred option.

When you break down your activities in this manner, you are able to come up with an idea of how you use your time. The above allocations can be listed as follows: -

24 HOURS

Sleep	8 hours
Getting Ready	1 hour
Commuting	1 hour (depending on location)
Working	8 hours
Eating and Sustenance	3 hours
Exercise	1 hour
Total2	2 hours

This calculation reveals that at the end of the day, once you have completed all your tasks you still have two hours left. These two hours offer some flexibility for recreational activities, additional rest, or to extend the working hours if necessary.

Understanding how you spend your time in a day, is the best way to begin to create strategies on how you can best utilize this time to get things done.

If you find that once you write down how you spend your day leads to time wastage, you can work on solution to improve the situation. The first solution would be to write down goals. Determine which part of your routine you would like to change and work towards amending it. Whether it is sleeping in late, taking extra breaks or waiting pointlessly, you can create a goal that addresses it.

Once you begin to plan your time, you will realize how valuable your time actually is. The result of this is that you will avoid filling up your schedule with pointless tasks that take away from your accomplishing your goals and getting things done.

Chapter 13
Loving All You Do to Get Things Done

Getting things done becomes substantially easier if you love all the things that you do. Life coaches around the world all seem to preach this message – once you love what you do you are able to accomplish amazing goals. This is because you have and built in motivation and a drive to fulfill your dreams and goals in a particular area.

People who love what they do display certain behaviors which are important to getting things done. These behaviors are: -

- Consistency

- Attention to Quality

- Results Oriented

- Deeply Motivated

- Determination

- A Positive Attitude

Consistency

People who love what they do are consistent in their attempt to meet their goals. They are willing to try and try again in order to get things done. For these people, giving up is not an option, because they are passionate about taking all the steps necessary to bring a plan to life.

When one reviews the way that they handle the work, what will be revealed is that they maintain a certain way of doing things, and their method will show a pattern where milestones are met, evaluations are done, and correction implemented along the way.

One of the advantages of working with someone who is consistent is that it becomes easy to refer back to what they have done in the past, and you can safely predict the avenue that they are likely to take in the future.

Attention to Quality

A person who loves what they do will always want to their very best. So people who pay attention to quality are able to get things done in the best way possible.

Quality follows closely with consistency. Whereas consistency looks at the person's ability to perfect their tasks over a period of time, quality is what is measured when looking at whether the executed tasks always meet the same standards.

Paying attention to quality can be a challenge, especially if one is working within a team. However, good quality work does not need to be redone or improved upon, and thus, it gets done much faster and better than if someone was simple being functional in fulfilling their work goals.

Results Oriented

In earlier chapters, a large amount of attention has been dedicated to results and how they are important when looking at getting things done. SMART goals were discussed as a way of measuring the results. Macro goals, micro goals and plans are also all about attaining results, and the result of time management is experiencing results.

A person who loves what they do will be results oriented. They are taking a particular path for a reason, and that reason is for them to meet their goals.

Through the love that they have for what they do, they are willing to go over all the obstacles and challenges that meet their goals.

Through the love that they have for what they do, they are willing to go over all the obstacles and challenges that may be encountered on the way to meeting these goals. They will therefore take the time to formulate strategies to overcome challenges, and to motivate the people whom they have to work with to ensure that they get things done.

Deeply Motivated

There are two types of motivation that have been addressed so far and those are intrinsic and extrinsic motivation. A person who loves what they are doing will have intrinsic motivation, although their motivation may be much deeper than would be expected of a person with intrinsic motivation.

Their motivation to get things done may be deep enough to become a part of their lifestyle. This means that it would be out of character for them to not get things done, especially when pursuing a goal that could lead to the fulfillment of a dream. So a healthy amount of energy is spent feeding this motivation so that it becomes easier to attain the desired results.

Determination

One who loves what they are doing will be determined to make sure they fulfill their tasks and goals. Determination basically refers to an attitude, one that insists that the goals can be met.

When one is determined, they will make sure that they have addressed each and every item on their daily checklist. They will be the first to volunteer should it be necessary for attaining their goals. A determined person will go out of their way and leaving their comfort zone to ensure that what needs to be done is done. It is through a deep love for the task at hand that determination is able to shine through.

A Positive Attitude

A coin has two sides, and every situation will always have two outlooks, that is a positive and negative one. People who love what they do opt to focus on a positive attitude. This means that they are always looking for better ways to accomplish their goals, and for the added benefits that they can receive from doing so. They are able to get things done due to a motivation to get excellent results, rather than being driven by a fear of failure.

Positive thinking has been attributed to getting results, and it applies when looking at getting things done. Believing that a task can be accomplished may be bring it close to expected fruition.

Chapter 14
Jumpstarting Productivity to Get *More* Things Done

Getting things done shouldn't be just about finishing a task. It should change the way you live your life, and give you a healthier and wealthier mindset. Once you have a healthier mindset, you will find that you can improve every aspect of your life, and overall, become a much more effective and efficient person. Fortunately, there are a lot of ways that you can become more productive in your everyday routine. It's up to you to take that step and incorporate these strategies into your lifestyle. Follow these productivity strategies to a tee, and you can expect your productivity to double in just a few weeks' time.

Create a work conducive environment

If your work environment doesn't encourage you to work, then you've just got your first hurdle to overcome. Your environment can set the stage for how well you work so if you don't see it as conducive, it's time to make a change. It is important to avoid a cluttered and overwhelming work environment that does not allow you to have a clear thought. Therefore, you should try and maintain a relatively neat or clean desk, by organizing your work into piles that you can easily reference. Experiment around to see what you like. Whether it's changing up the room color or putting on a few inspirational wall art, don't be afraid to explore what you need to do to get your productivity up.

First things first

Even though you may feel like you have a million things to do every day, make sure that you accomplish the most important tasks first. Accomplishing the important things first can set your day and establish whether you've been productive for the day or not. It is on these tasks that you should spend the most time, allocating enough time to them to avoid feeling rushed or under pressure. Next time you feel like you're underachieving, reprioritize your tasks list and move in on the important ones. Once they are completed, your mind will be free to adequately go through your other tasks.

Apply the 80/20 rule

The 80/20 rule states that 80% of output is the product of 20% effort. The other 20% output will be achieved by the remaining 80% effort. So how can this help improve your productivity? It teaches you to let go of the nitty gritty details and concentrate on the first 20% of effort that you put into your work. This really comes down to time management and how you have prioritized your work. You can leave the many tedious yet minor tasks to the end of our work day.

Update your skills

Working on your limitations is an effective way to be more productive overall. Therefore you should take advantage of any training opportunities that are availed to you. If possible, enroll in an after work course that will teach you new skills. The amount of time that you spend studying your new skills may seem counterproductive, but once you get the hang of your new skills, you'll be able to finish more in a shorter span of time. This is especially true if you work on your time management, efficiency or organization skills. Think of your skillset as your tool to get better at your field. Take every opportunity to ensure that you're always ahead of the game.

Reclaim your mornings

This may depend on the individual, but if you really want to increase your productivity, it's worth give a try. Most of us are most productive in the morning, after our minds have had the benefit of resting through a good night's sleep. Waking earlier that you normally would gives you more time to do things for yourself. This becomes even easier if you go to sleep earlier so that you can get an adequate amount of rest. Reclaim your mornings to exercise, meditate, or cook a healthy breakfast for yourself. Many people skip breakfast due to being in a hurry to start their activities for the day, but extensive research has revealed that breakfast is the most important meal of the day as it gives you a much needed boost to get started with your tasks at hand. Exercise will get your blood flowing around your body, increasing your concentration and energy levels. Meditation will help you to clearly your mind so that it is easier to focus on the tasks at hand. Do whatever you want, as long it gets you in the zone and improve your mood. Also, the quietness of the mornings can be a conducive in getting more things done. You'll have time to regroup your thoughts and set your goals for the day.

Never Procrastinate Again

Procrastination is a phenomenon that happens to every one of us. One minute you find yourself doing your work, and the next you find that you're looking at e-mail or chatting on the phone with a friend. However, it's not the distractions that are making you late on your work, whether it is homework or something your boss needs within the next three hours. It's your brain telling you to stop doing something because it's too much for you to handle.

Just before you found something else to do, you may have experienced an increased heart rate, you were suddenly thirsty, or your palms grew sweaty. All of these signals are signs of stress happening within your body because you are mentally telling yourself you can't do whatever it is you need to get done. It could have been poor planning on your part or maybe your boss didn't allow you enough time to get this project done, but it's happened. You're now fifteen minutes away from your deadline and there is no possible way you're going to get it finished.

This reaction within our bodies is normal; however, it can be detrimental to our personal lives, careers, and education. The good news is, there are ways you can prevent this from happening. But first, you must look out for the warning signs in order to understand what you are doing when you are procrastinating.

Read on to find out the different warning signs you may be exhibiting that let you know you're already or you're going to procrastinate.

Chapter One
Understanding the Warning Signs

Warning Signs

Waiting for Perfect

You've told yourself you need equipment, time, space, music, whatever it may be. Then you sit back and you wait for it to magically appear while you're texting your friends or playing a game on your cell phone. Waiting for the perfect environment or the perfect tools to get the job done is never going to be a valid excuse. If you truly need something, then ask or find it.

No Strain, No Gain

You believe you work best while you're under pressure; however, studies have shown that people who work under pressure make more mistakes and their brains are always in a state of beta waves. Beta waves are the frequency within the brain between twenty-two to thirty-eight Hertz, meaning it's very quick.

Let's use an example. A person who knows they have to get away from a predator quickly using their intelligence will subconsciously send their mind into beta waves. They're on the edge, high energy, and stressed at the same time. While this state of mind is okay for a short period of time, the proverbial gazelle outrunning the lion has a break right after their short burst. Putting your brain into overload like this for a long period of time can be detrimental to your health and mental well-being.

Productive Procrastination

We've all done it.

'But I have to do this because it's more important', or 'I had all these other tasks to do and you expected me to do that?'

Using other tasks that are, in reality, less important than the one you were given is a cop-out. You're using those tasks as an excuse when you could have done them after you got your time sensitive work finished. When you go to do something else, ask yourself if it's really more important than what you're currently doing, and be honest when you answer.

Second Guessing

Everyone goes through a time when they're unsure of themselves; however, that's not a valid excuse for not getting work done! Check it once to be sure there are no glaring errors and hand it in. Nothing in this world is perfect and second guessing your decisions or your work all day long is only going to make it worse, not better.

Lack of Knowledge or Skills

A deficit in skills or knowledge is a very common reason for procrastinating. If you lack the knowledge or skills in order to complete a task, you're going to put that task off for as long as possible. For example, if you're not a good reader but your boss hands you several articles you have to read in order to get the project done, you're going to put it off as long as you possibly can before you torment yourself with reading. In fact, some people put off projects because they don't want to admit to themselves that they have a lack of skill in that area of expertise and they don't want to be seen as dumb.

Sometimes, seeing someone else who can point out *why* you are procrastinating can help. Seeing a counselor if this problem is affecting your life in a severely negative way might be a good idea because he or she will be able to tell you where you need to improve. Then they can help you find someone or point out courses you can take in order to feel more confident about your skill sets.

It's Boring

Unfortunately, not everything in life is going to be as exciting as skydiving out of a plane, or even as exciting as sipping a freshly brewed cup of coffee or another favorite beverage. It's going to be like eating cardboard for lunch, but sometimes we have to do things that are boring in order to succeed in life. Not many people like to clean, but they just do it because they don't want to live in a messy home.

Sometimes the best answer is to just do what you have to do in order to get through your class or your workday, and go home and enjoy something without that cloud of guilt hanging over you.

Lack of Motivation

There is a common misbelief that if you don't feel motivated to do a task, then you shouldn't have to do that task or there might be something wrong with you. Let's look at a few examples of things that you may not feel motivated to do, but they are things you should be doing such as doing your taxes, mowing the lawn, going grocery shopping, scrubbing the toilet, or any other mundane task you can think of that you don't really want to do.

According to psychologists, motivation actually comes from starting the task. Once you begin the task, you'll feel motivated to continue it and you will finish it. Sometimes it takes a little more than just the reward of finishing, but that will be discussed in a later chapter.

Lack of motivation may also come from a bad attitude. You may think that something is stupid or that it's unnecessary. Take a step back from the situation and evaluate what you thought when you didn't start the task you know you have to complete. Were you putting it down because you don't want to do it? If you were, then think about how this task will help you in the long run. By completing a course assignment, will you pass the test and be able to obtain your degree? Or perhaps if you complete this assignment from your boss you will be closer to a promotion?

Think of the long run, not just the present.

Fear of Failure

This is worse than second guessing. This is that heart pounding, stress inducing fear that makes you step away from the task you were about to do and find something else to do, and find it quickly. Fear of failure is the main reason a lot of people procrastinate.

You might tell yourself that if you do not try, then the failing grade or anger from your boss is not really justified because you didn't really try. If you actually put in your best effort and end up getting the same result, then that reflects even worse on you, in your opinion.

For example, you may have a test you know is coming up, but instead of studying for it, you put it off until the last second and cram the night before. If you end up getting a bad grade on the test, you can tell yourself that if you'd had more time, then you would have done better on the test. Or perhaps you had a paper due and you decided to delay until the last day to get it done, or you are even late with the paper. You might tell yourself that you could have gotten a better grade if you'd had more time.

By procrastinating in this manner, we're giving ourselves a payoff that makes us not look like a failure in our own eyes. Sometimes we'll fill our time with busy work in order to have a legitimate reason for not getting the work done, but in reality, we were just avoiding the task altogether.

Unfortunately, fear of failure may stem from our upbringing. Perfectionism can be a detrimental, psychological illness that is fostered by a childhood environment with high expectations and no room for mistakes. Parents can set standards so high that not even they could live up to them, but they expect their son or daughter to do so. These high standards can actually cause a person to freeze up mentally and they will do anything to get out of the task because they believe they cannot do it.

Their self-esteem, self-worth, and internal voice are all so negative that nothing they can ever do will be good enough for anyone. People who have this problem need to seek out help right away from a professional because that type of thinking can lead to serious, mental illnesses later on such as depression, anxiety, and ADHD.

Fear of Success

It might seem silly when you read it, but fear of success is another common cause of procrastination. You may be thinking that if you complete a project exceptionally well, then the instructor or boss will want you to do just as well or even better the next time. Another fear might be that you will be recognized for your success and being an introvert, you don't want the spotlight. You would much rather stay in the background.

While this may seem like the opposite of fear of failure, they're actually tied to the same thing, your self-worth. If your self-worth and self-esteem are tied to your successes rather than who you are as a person, then you will fear not being able to be good enough the next time. If your self-worth is tied to whether or not you are good enough, you will put off the task in order to avoid that potential success or failure.

Rebellion

Perhaps you're going to college because you know you're going to work in the family business afterward, and your parents are paying for your education only if you take a certain course. However, you've decided you're not as interested in that course as you once were and you'd like to branch off to another subject. When you bring this up with your parents, you may be told that you're going to finish a degree you're earning because they're in control of the situation. This leads to you handing in assignments late, earning low grades on purpose, and flunking courses.

Maybe your instructor or boss offended you in some way or angered you, and you are retaliating by not getting things done. These tactics can often be used on other classmates or teammates and parents, too. The important thing to remember here is that you are only hurting yourself and ultimately, you are the one who loses.

By rebelling, you are reacting and not acting; therefore, your behavior's control is actually resting with whomever you are trying to rebel against rather than with yourself. If your parents are telling you to do something, tune them out and ask yourself if this is the right course for your life. Don't let their decisions weigh in on yours.

By recognizing that you are procrastinating, you can now move on to take actionable steps that will help you stop the procrastination and get your work done in a timely manner.

Chapter Two
Change Your Environment

The first thing you're going to need to do after you've recognized why you are procrastinating is to change your environment. If you study in the dorm room or common area, try changing your environment by studying at the park or in the library. Choose a quiet place that will hold fewer distractions.

So why do you need to do this? And why would you need to change your environment more than once?

Changing your environment actually has an impact on your productivity. Sometimes an environment will become less effective because you're bored with it, so don't be afraid to change it around or even move to a completely new location in your building or house. If you see a new office open up at work, think about how you'd like it and if you think you would, then ask your boss politely if you can have it.

Ask yourself these questions about your workspace:

- Does it make you want to work?

- Is it distracting?

If you answered yes to the second question, then you need to seriously consider revamping that workspace. You need to be sure to pick the right workspace, if you can, in order to get your work done. If you're stuck at a stationary desk and you're unable to change your space, then you can make your desk feel like home. Tidy it up and put pictures where you can seem them from your peripheral vision. If you have a green thumb, add some plants. Even buying one of those little eco-system pots that have lights in order to maintain a plant will help. You don't have to have natural light for a plant.

The next step is making sure your workspace is organized so it is conducive with work. If you're workspace is mess, you're going to feel sluggish and disorganized. If you have a nice, tidy workspace, you'll feel energized and inspired to get your work done. Some people claim clutter makes them feel better, but in reality, it doesn't. Human beings like to know where their tools are so that they can easily access them. Clutter brings in stress, which will lead to procrastination.

The following are five steps that will help you reduce clutter and get organized in your workspace.

Step One

Remove everything from your room. When I say everything, I mean it. Find the junk in the cupboards and hidden in the corners and place them all into boxes as if you're moving from one state to another. Then get down to the nitty gritty and clean your workspace by vacuuming, mopping, cleaning walls, cleaning the cubicle, and organizing any wires you may not be able to remove.

This could be the last time that you are able to clean up your environment for a while, so be thorough.

Step Two

View all the items in your workspace or room as equal. Meaning, if you have furniture in there, that is prat of your clutter. Don't discount anything because you think it's too big to move or it's a surface rather than an item. Everything in that room or workspace is potential clutter and has to be removed. Besides, you might find some junk or things you need under that furniture or in that cabinet.

It's very easy for your mind to bypass the furniture and surfaces and head straight for the junk piled in or on the furniture and on the surfaces. However, you have to be sure to consider everything as you're removing items.

Step Three

Choose the absolute necessities. There are items in your workspace that you really don't need to use more than once a month or even once a year. Find another spot in the office or your home for those objects and only bring in the items you're going to need daily. Remember to choose wisely and when you do use those items, return them to the closet or other space from which they came!

Step Four

Once you've made the decision about what is coming back into the workspace and what will not be returning, be sure to put just as much thought into where those items are going. Switch up where they had gone before to make things seem fresh and new, and make sure you're putting the items in easily accessible areas. For instance, you want your stapler to be in a drawer if you don't use it often, but it has to be right at your desk when you need it. Try to organize everything in drawers neatly and even get yourself some organization equipment.

There are special drawer inserts that will hold pens, paperclips, staplers, and other assorted items you may need in your office. Buy yourself a pen holder so that they're not rolling around your desk. Even make sure that your pictures are in view but out of your way. Every item has a specific place and you should make sure to put just as much thought into where you're putting it as to why you kept it in the first place.

Step Five

Commit to a regular decluttering.

You've found a new attitude and you think that you're going to put everything back into its place after you've used it. Until, that is, you are called into a meeting and drop a pen on your desk without thinking. You tell yourself you'll get it later, but you end up not. Then the stapler is not in its place, or you have a sticky note stack piling up on your desk. Clutter is going to happen to the best of us. It creeps up slowly and all of a sudden it's like there's a mountain of things you have to put away.

If you set aside five minutes at the end of every day or an hour at the end of a workweek to declutter your space, clutter will not creep back in. You have to make a conscious decision to declutter at regular intervals in order to keep your workspace clean.

Now that you have a workspace that is decluttered and makes you feel productive, let's get started on your third step to getting your work done: making long-term goals.

Chapter Three
Create Long-Term Goals

Long-term goals are the backbone of your plan to get your work done on time. These goals can be either twenty-four hours or up to ten years later depending upon what they are for. However, figuring out how to make these long-term goals can be a task all in and of itself.

The first thing you need to do is ask yourself if you are taking the correct steps to get your project or task done. If you are not, gather your thoughts and maintain focus. So what is focus?

Focus is centering your thoughts and attention onto a specific task, object, or activity for a length of time. In order to maintain focus, you should think about short-term, small tasks and goals because you will see the results quicker and your motivation levels will remain high. If you are focusing on the long-term project end result, then you will quickly lose your focus and motivation.

It's also more difficult to measure the progress on long-term goals rather than short-term ones, so we'll discuss how to break down your long-term goals into short-term ones in the next chapter. But first, get comfortable in your workspace and bring out a calendar, whether it's digital or paper, and start to think about the large steps you need to do in order to get your project completed.

Define the Meaningfully

Make sure that the long-term goals you are defining are meaningful and try to think about them in a positive light. Perhaps your long-term goal is not to complete this project, but completing this project will lead you to one of your long-term goals such as getting a promotion, raise, or obtaining a higher education. Your long-term goals do not have to end with this project. In fact, if you're not excited about the project, then it should not be the end long-term goal.

When you pick out your end long-term goal, make sure it's something you are excited about and want to complete. Be sure it's something you are passionate about and eager to accomplish rather than something that is dull and boring to you. Once you're doing picking out your goal, make sure to make a list of what you will obtain if you complete that goal. That is your reward and motivation.

Write Down Long-Term Goals

As you are doing this, be sure to write down your goals! Sometimes, life gets in the way of our long-term goals and we end up missing one or forgetting about it completely. Put them in a place where you will see them daily such as on your bathroom mirror, the refrigerator, or in your cubicle at work. You want to keep your goals in your sight frequently in order to remind yourself to complete the small tasks that will lead you to those rewards at the end.

Set Reminders

Set a reminder on your phone or your computer in order to get you to look at your goals if they're not in an obvious sight path. Even make a Treasure Map that will put you on the right path to achieving your goals. By making it fun, you will feel less stress about completing a task and procrastination will go to the wayside.

Strengthen Self-Regulation

This is the ability to control your emotions and impulses, and is one of the most important factors in obtaining your goals. The first thing you have to do is work on your self-discipline. This will help you continuously move forward and work hard even when you're feeling like procrastinating. Self-discipline will help you move forward with your goals, and it will lead to self-regulation.

Self-regulation is when you believe you are able to complete your goals internally. You no longer need an external push from someone else to get those goals completed because you believe in yourself. This is where self-esteem comes into play. You have to believe that you are responsible for your own success, and that you can achieve it.

Set Aside Time

It's simple to put a little list on your computer screen or organize those long-term goals in a calendar, but when are you going to find the time to complete these goals? You have to set aside daily or weekly time in order to get these goals completed. So if you have a project, set aside a block of time to work on it daily in order to finish it by the due date.

You may have to change around habits or other tasks that are less important in order to complete these long-term goals, so start making short-term goals that will get you closer to where you need to be. Be sure to set aside time during the part of the day when you are most productive. So if you are a morning person who gets most of their work done before noon, then set aside time during this slot of your day for your long-term goals. If you find you work better at night, then rearrange your schedule so that you can get the work done then.

Stay on Course

Even the best of us find ourselves straying off the main course of our goals. It's very easy to let life get in the way of what we want to do with it, so be sure to set up those reminders and keep a steady eye on the prize. If you have new ideas for where you want to go in life, write them down and don't take any action until you're absolutely sure that's where you want to go.

At the very least, sleep on any new ideas and think about them in the morning. You may find yourself surprised that something the day before that seems like an excellent idea was really a terrible one.

Now that you're able to create long-term goals, let's take a look at creating smaller, short-term goals that will help you get to those long-term goals.

Chapter Four
Break Down the Long –Term Goals into Short-Term Goals

Short term goals are goals that can completed within a twelve month timeframe, or a goal that could be completed the day you set it. They're smaller steps you need to take in order to get to a larger, long-term goal. For instance, if you are a student and you know you have to get a paper written that you don't feel particularly excited about, remind yourself that the paper you are writing is going to get you to your long-term goal of obtaining a degree.

These goals are the smaller, more obtainable steps that you know you can get done if you set your mind to it. Long-term goals may seem more difficult to obtain and that is why they should be broken down into shorter term goals. So how do you break them down into baby steps?

Focusing on the Long-Term Goal

First you have to be sure that you have a long-term goal that you can focus on. So write it down at the top of a piece of paper and be sure that's where you want to be in five or ten years. For example, the long-term goal will be that promotion into manager of your department or obtaining that education.

Your long-term goal is a statement of your hopes and dreams. It is your passion and your meaning in life. Get excited about it or change the goal if you can't.

Break the Long-Term into Short-Term

Now that you are focused on that long-term goal, what are the short-term goals you need to accomplish before you can finish the larger goal? For example, if you know you have a research paper due by Friday and it's Monday, you have short-term goals of research, organizing information, creating an outline, and writing.

Perhaps by Thursday morning you want to have a first draft finished and by Thursday evening you want that draft polished and edited. Those are short-term goals.

Another example might be if you want to obtain a promotion and you know you need to accomplish a few tasks before you get it, like upping your sales in your department by twenty-five percent and showing up to work on time. Those are your short-term goals.

Evaluating Short-Term Goals

Now that you've broken down your steps, evaluate them. Make sure that they are all conducive to where you want to be in life and they all pertain to your long-term goal. Once you've completed a short-term goal, go ahead and check it off the list, but don't forget about it!

You'll want to go back and evaluate how you got that goal accomplished and what you can do better in the future, if anything.

Rewards

Just as with long-term goals, you should reward yourself with short-term goals. You'll need further incentive to keep going, so take some time for yourself and relax. We all need to reenergize at some point, and taking those few moments can help you get a clear picture of where you stand pertaining to your goals.

Maintain a Positive Attitude

Throughout this entire experience, you have to be sure that you are paying attention to your health both mentally and physically. Get enough rest, eat healthy, and exercise daily in order to keep your attitude above the line rather than below. How you feel about what you are doing is the most important part to avoiding procrastination.

So let's take a look at a long-term goal broken down into short-term goals as an example.

Long-Term Goal: Complete an Essay Assignment

- **Short-Term Goal #1:** Come up with a thesis and decide on an outline.

- **Short-Term Goal #2:** Research quotes and studies that pertain to the sections in the outline.

- Short-Term Goal #3: Begin writing.

- **Short-Term Goal #4:** Finish first draft and edit.

- **Short-Term Goal #5:** Complete the final draft.

Notice that these are just steps the student needs to take to obtain the long-term goal of completing an essay assignment. There aren't any timeframes put on those steps because they will come during the actionable steps process in the following chapter.

Chapter Five
Break Down Those Short-Term Goals into Actionable Steps

We procrastinate because we're subconsciously thinking about that long-term goal and even the short-term goals can seem overwhelming. Where are we going to find the time and what if we don't like the subject matter? Well, if you create actionable steps in order to complete those short-term goals, you'll have somewhere to start.

The first thing, when you are breaking down short-term goals, is to set aside a chunk of time daily in order to work on that short-term goal. Be sure that your short-term goals are accomplishable and reasonable, and then continue with your actionable steps.

The second step is to rid yourself of distractions during those actionable steps. Common distractions and how to get rid of them will be discussed in chapter six.

The final step with actionable steps is rewarding yourself with a small reward after you've completed each one. Think of this as if you are training a dog or you are trying to learn a new habit. You have to give your brain something to feel good about, so eat a piece of candy or play games for half an hour after you've completed an actionable step. This will keep you feeling motivated.

So let's take an example from chapter four with the long-term goal of completing an essay assignment.

Long-Term Goal: Complete an Essay Assignment

- **Short-Term Goal #1:** Come up with a thesis and decide on an outline.

  - ✓ **Actionable Step A:** Research the topic at the library from 6PM to 7PM Monday evening.
  - ✓ **Actionable Step B:** Complete the outline at the library from 7PM to 8PM Monday evening.
- **Short-Term Goal #2:** Research quotes and studies that pertain to the sections in the outline.

  - ✓ **Actionable Step A:** Find books at the public library from 7PM to 7:30PM on Tuesday evening.
  - ✓ **Actionable Step B:** Find quotes in research books at the library from 7:30PM to 8:30PM.
  - ✓ **Actionable Step C:** Research information online from 8:30PM to 9:30PM at the library.
- Short-Term Goal #3: Begin writing.

  - ✓ **Actionable Step A:** Set aside time from 6PM to 8PM on Wednesday evening to start writing.
- **Short-Term Goal #4:** Finish first draft and edit.

  - ✓ **Actionable Step A:** Finish the first draft from 6AM to 8AM Thursday to finish the first draft.
  - ✓ **Actionable Step B:** Set aside time from 12PM to 2PM Thursday to edit the first draft and mark mistakes.
- **Short-Term Goal #5:** Complete the final draft.

  - ✓ **Actionable Step A:** Set aside time from 6PM to 9PM Thursday evening to go back and correct mistakes and rewrite.
  - ✓ **Actionable Step B:** Reward with an hour at the movies with friends.

By this point, you should have a definitive plan as to what you are going to do and when you are going to do it. Focus on those small, actionable steps that are achievable and make sure to complete them during the allotted time. If you find you need more time to complete a task, schedule it in immediately.

Unfortunately, no matter how much we schedule and how excited we are about a project, sometime we run into distractions. The next chapter will discuss how to eliminate or alleviate some of the more common distractions people complain about.

Chapter Six
Eliminate Distractions

Distractions are so easy to come by when we're not focused on our goals or we're feeling procrastination creeping in on us. The most common distraction people discuss is electronic distractions. These include emails, phone messages or phone calls, instant messaging, and the internet. Thankfully, there are some simple steps you can take to eliminate these distractions from your work zone in order to buckle down and get what you need to get done, done.

E-Mail

Most office workers or freelancers could spend all day answering e-mails that both pertain to work and do not. Everyone seems to want to share something or ask for something to be completed, but none of it really pertains to what we're doing in that moment. E-mails are an excellent tool for communication, but sometimes we need to shut that communication down.

Schedule a time to check your e-mails and let people who may send you an urgent message that you have specific times you will be available. As an example, you could check your e-mail when you first arrive at work, at lunch, and right before you leave with half hour slots allotted to check at those times. In addition, remove any apps from your desktop that alert you when you have a message. You want to keep them out of your sight and be sure to turn off any noises, too. These are extremely distracting and pull you right out of your zone of concentration.

When you schedule times to check your e-mails, make sure it's at a time when you are not too busy. Pick those low productivity times during the day because you want to use your high productivity times for your more important work. Chatting with people through e-mail does not take a lot of effort on your part or theirs, so be sure to put e-mail discussions in an appropriate time slot.

If an e-mail will take more time than just a few minutes to respond to or you need to turn that e-mail into something you have to do, find an empty slot or create one on your calendar and pencil it in. Remember to keep that e-mail program closed when you are not checking it and avoid the temptation to open it up when you feel stressed or upset about your goals. You need to evaluate your stress and face it head on rather than finding something else to do.

Another awesome tip is to set your e-mail program to manual. That means you have to hit a refresh button to send or receive e-mails, so you will not be constantly bombarded with new ones. When you are feeling relaxed and comfortable, you can check those e-mails.

Instant Messaging

The invention of cell phones was amazing, and they've been very helpful to society; however, they're also detrimental when they're used in the wrong manner. Just like anything else that requires communication, instant messaging can be a large distraction to people who are trying to get a goal accomplished. Unfortunately, cell phones are an excellent way for coworkers, friends, or spouses to interrupt us from our work. Their intentions might be good, but they're being destructive toward your life.

If you have to use instant messaging to talk with someone, make sure your queries are short and sweet. Do not spend too much time chitchatting, and if the issue is more complex, make a phone call or send an e-mail at the appropriate time. You can also turn off instant messaging on your computer and your phone if you feel the need to disappear for a time with your online presence.

If there are specific people who may need to contact you using these two methods, instant messaging or texting, then make sure they know the hours that you are available to talk. Unless it's a complete emergency from your boss, you're going to want to keep these methods of communication to a minimum.

Phone Calls and Voicemail Messages

For some of us, phone calls are the essence of our work. For example, you may be a real estate agent and that phone call could be a client calling to sign a contract. While this is important, that client can wait a few hours in order for you to get other work accomplished. It's best to treat phone calls and voicemails just like instant messaging and e-mails. Turn it off when you have to and only turn it back one when you are finished with your work.

If you have children and feel the need to leave your phone on in case of an emergency, then do so, but make sure your coworkers, friends, and family understand that phone calls during certain times should only be made if it's a dire situation. Allow all phone calls during those times to go to voicemail and then listen to that voice mail when you are wrapping up a task.

Only listen to a voicemail right away if it's from someone you know might have an emergency, like a child or your boss.

The Internet

The internet is a wonderful tool that is used and abused by many procrastinators. It's so easy to just open up an internet tab and start perusing the web for 'information' you think you may need or just to take a load off for five minutes. Before you know it, you've been staring at that web page for more than half an hour reading information that doesn't pertain to what you were supposed to be doing. It's a wealth of useful and non-useful information and should be treated like a tool to get work done rather than an intellectual playground.

If you want to read the news, treat it like people used to treat newspapers twenty years ago. Grab a cup of coffee in the morning before work and read the news. Then set it aside for the rest of the work day and read it in the evening sometime before bed.

Close the internet browser immediately after you find the information you need. If you're constantly going to social media network websites like Facebook and Twitter, try blocking those sites from your computer for a while. You could also try logging out and telling your computer to not remember the password. By taking those extra few seconds to have to type in a password, you've given yourself enough time to feel guilty and stop your actions.

There are actually programs out there that you can obtain such as Freedom and Anti-Social that will allow you to set up times where you cannot get onto certain websites. Then, at the end of the day, you will be able to get back on them.

Perhaps at lunch you can take a short internet break. Look at the internet for half an hour and then get back to work. This acts as a small reward for you doing your work when you were supposed to, but be sure it doesn't go too far.

Co-Workers

Along with communication come the other people on the other end of that communication channel. Co-workers can be the greatest distraction from work that we're supposed to be doing, but there are several ways to avoid these interruptions.

Close the Door

If you feel that a coworker is coming into your office too much and you happen to have a door, try closing it in order to get some peace. If the person knocks or decides to come in despite the door being close, and then let them know that you closed the door for a reason in a polite way. You don't want to upset them, but let them know that you are easily distracted by interruptions and you have to get back to work. In addition to this, you can try putting a sign on your door letting people know that you're busy.

Sometimes, when you're a manager, you have to have your door proverbially always open to the employees beneath you. Try to work from home on large projects or hide in a conference room when you don't want to be disturbed. Let them know that you have a lot of work to get done and that they shouldn't disturb you unless it's an emergency. However, be sure to set aside time where you are free to talk with employees about any problems they may be having.

Use Headphones

You don't have to turn anything on, but if you have headphones in, people are less likely to disturb you. They think you are listening to music or you may be listening to something important, so they tend to go away and come back at a different time. If music or noise distracts you, just keep the headphones off and treat them like a pair of earplugs.

Talk to Your Disruptor

You may be in a cubicle where you have to share the space with someone else, and that person may decide that you are a good person to talk with whenever they wish. In a polite way that doesn't offend them, let them know that they're distracting you. Make a joke about your short attention span or set aside time to walk with them at lunch that way they don't feel ignored.

If someone consistently comes into your office or your cubicle and sits down on an empty spot on your desk or in a vacant chair, try putting a stack of papers there or a coffee cup. This will politely keep them from sitting down and staying to chat for too long. In addition, try standing up and going to the water cooler to get a drink, and then end the conversation gently by letting them know you have to get back to work.

Work Environment

As discussed before, sometimes your work environment is your distraction. You may have windows, a busy highway outside, or loud co-workers that can't seem to find the time to be quiet. All of these distractions can add up and they can be very stressful when you're trying to get your work done.

Work in a Different Location

If the window is a problem and you constantly find you are looking out it then try finding another workspace. Let your boss know the problem or simply shift your computer to another end of the desk that isn't as close to the window.

White Noise

If you can't seem to find peace and quiet in the workplace due to noise problems then try buying a white noise machine that will cover any annoying sounds. You can use headphones with these in order to not disrupt your colleagues, too. There are even downloads that have white noise in the background and you can set them to repeat while you're blocking unwanted sounds.

Other Projects or Tasks

You know how you can't seem to go to bed at night and you're always thinking of other things to do? Stop doing that.

First you need to create a to-do list and organize it from top priority to low priority. Then you have to stick to that to-do list. Track your day and stick to it. You could discover you're spending hours dealing with interruptions and faux emergencies from coworkers, friends, and family.

Learn how to delegate your tasks if you can. If you need the trash taken out at home, but you have a project you really have to get done, ask a family member to do it kindly if you can. Delegation is a tool used by many successful people, so learn how to use it.

Fatigue

Being tired can be a terrible distraction. If you're constantly working in the beta mindset discussed earlier, you will tire yourself out quickly. To eliminate fatigue from your daily life, try these following steps.

Get enough sleep the previous night. Many people only get four to six hours of sleep a night when you really need seven to eight. Set aside a specific bed time and stick with it no matter what. If you find you're having trouble getting to sleep, try to do some exercises in order to make yourself physically tired. Sometimes sitting in a chair all day is mentally tiring, but our bodies still have too much energy to go to bed. In addition, try meditating in order to calm your restless mind. You might be thinking of all the things you have to do tomorrow, so stop doing that by sending your brain wave patterns into the theta waves. These are the waves that we experience just before we fall asleep.

If all else fails, count sheep. It may seem silly, but counting sheep or counting anything else jumping over a fence will keep your mind busy and allow it to fall asleep.

If you're getting enough sleep, you may be experiencing dehydration because you're too focused on what you're doing. Try to set aside times to get up from the office chair and get a small drink at the water cooler. Make sure it's a quick trip and don't get stuck conversing with coworkers. This will also give your mind a break for a few minutes, too.

Sometimes going for a walk will reenergize you and getting some fresh air will make you feel more alert. Being sedentary for a long time actually makes us mentally and physically tired, but stretching those muscles will awaken your mind.

In addition to getting exercise and obtaining enough sleep, you may want to consider looking at your diet. Some foods will be more energizing than others, and sometimes we rely too much on coffee and other caffeinated beverages to keep us going. Utilizing those beverages too much will make us more susceptible to crashing, so try to limit your caffeine intake and reduce it when you do drink coffee or tea.

Now that you know how to eliminate some of those pesky distractions, you can move on to knowing how to reward yourself when you are doing your work on time and efficiently.

Chapter Seven
Bargaining with Yourself

If you have children, think about how you might get them to do their homework. You might be a parent who rewards them with a snack or free time later on if they get their homework done on time, or you might be one of those parents who punishes the child and uses that as motivation. Both of those are called extrinsic or external motivations. They push us or our children to do something in order to get a good or avoid a bad result.

Studies have shown that children who already had an intrinsic or internal motivation do not benefit from an external motivation later on because they get too used to the external motivation and no longer harbor an internal one. Therefore, using an external motivation should only be during the occurrence when there is something that you already do not want to do, such as completing a task that will lead to you completing a short-term goal.

This means that if you enjoy the researching aspect of completing an essay paper or a project for work, then do not reward yourself with a special food or play time when you are finished. This will only desensitize you toward that reward, and you'll end up back where you started when you're finished.

In addition, you want your rewards to be synonymous with what you are accomplishing. Thus, if you have a goal where you want to complete the research phase and you hate researching, then have a few pieces of candy after you're finished with that goal. Once you've completed the long-term goal of finishing an essay on time, you can celebrate with something larger like going to the movies with friends.

Here are some examples of rewards that you can give to yourself if you complete a small task or short-term goal:

- Take a hot bubble bath

- Order your favorite food

- Go to the movies

- Watch an episode of your favorite TV show

- Take a nap

- Get ice cream

- Buy a lottery ticket

Here are some examples of rewards that you can give to yourself once you've completed a short-term goal only:

- Buy new clothes

- Take a weekend to yourself or go away on vacation for a few days

- Get a massage

- Take yourself or friends out to dinner

Here are some examples of rewards you can give to yourself once you've completed a long-term goal:

- Take a weekend cruise

- Get a tech gadget

- Go shopping

- Go to a spa

- Buy something you've always wanted

Now that you understand the concept of rewards and different reward levels let's move on to vividly imagining yourself completing those goals and getting those rewards.

Chapter Eight
Vividly Imagining Finishing the Goal

People are visual creatures and we can use that to our advantage. We can trick ourselves into being motivated to do something when we visualize what we are going to accomplish and how we are going to accomplish it. If thinking about the end result and the entire goal being overexcites you, then think about how that will feel.

Use the five different senses to make this image in your mind as real as possible.

Sight

You want to make sure the images you are imagining are bright and vivid. Even exaggerate them a little in order to get the point across to your mind that this is really great.

Smell

If one of your rewards is going to be going on vacation or going out to dinner, imagine how that's going to smell. Inhale deeply your favorite food's aroma or a bunch of flowers at the spa.

Sound

Imagine that you are at a restaurant or you're buying your favorite object at a store. What does that sound like? Listen to the sound of people around you and the clatter of forks on plates. Listen to how your friends are telling you you're great for accomplishing one of your long-term goals.

Touch

Touch the fork in front of you at the restaurant. Touch the object you're going to buy after you accomplish your goal and feel the weight of it in your hands. Feel the paper of the essay you're handing into your instructor when you complete it. Make sure that you're really imagining how it's going to physically feel.

Taste

If you're at a favorite restaurant or having a favorite candy when you're finished with your goal, imagine how it tastes. Remember the texture of the food as you're swallowing it and really put yourself into the image.

By doing these five things, you are creating a mental image of how it will be like when you finish your goal. Be sure that everything is positive and abolish any negative thoughts as these will inhibit your ability to perform.

Chapter Nine
Listing Consequences

For some people, focusing on the negative of what will happen if you don't accomplish a task is a better route to go. Imagine that you did not complete a project on time for your boss or that you didn't hand in an essay when it was do. Now, list five consequences of those actions.

Some examples might be:

- Being fired

- Being kicked out of class

- Not graduating college

- Not getting a promotion

- Ridicule

By focusing on the consequences, you will empower yourself to move forward and get what you need to get done quicker. However, if this step makes you feel like not finishing your goals, then skip it. Some people deal better with positive reinforcement rather than negative.

Chapter Ten
Asking Someone to Help and Making your Intentions Public

Asking Someone to Help

Sometimes we just need a person to help us complete a task. Perhaps you're starting your own business or you're completing an essay but you just don't know where to start. Ask an instructor or ask a mentor who has been in the business before to help you. Sometimes your peers can be an excellent tool to getting you where you want to go. Just be sure that they're not a distraction and they really are helping you.

In addition, be sure that the person you ask to help is not someone who is always negative. You need to surround yourself with people who are a positive influence on you. No one wants to hang around a Negative Nancy, so be sure to avoid them at all costs.

Making Intentions Public

By going public with what you are doing, you are opening the door for positive people to come into your life to help you. You're also inviting the negative inside, so be aware to filter people's words and their intentions.

In addition to opening the door for others to enter your project, you are making it very difficult for yourself to get out of your goals without losing face. Sometimes, outward influences gently reminding us to do something are the best way to go. We're allowing others to support us and we're feeling the weight of getting something done on time in order to not look like a failure.

However, sometimes making intentions public is the wrong route to do. You have to judge whether or not you're someone who will feel empowered by this or if you will feel too stressed about it and start procrastinating.

Conclusion

Remember that procrastination is a normal feeling and an emotion that everyone feels in their lifetime. You're not always going to want to complete a task that will lead to something greater because you're looking at your hand in front of you rather than looking at the road ahead and what it holds. In order to be someone who does not procrastinate, you have to create long-term goals and think about the future ahead of you rather than the mundane task you might have to complete right now.

Remember the following when you are faced with a project that you do not want to complete:

1. Ask yourself how this project will help you in the future in obtaining your long-term goals of completing an education or obtaining a raise.

2. Eliminate distractions around you by turning off electronics or even turning off the WIFI on those electronics.

3. Politely let coworkers know that you are busy or other students.

4. Reward yourself along the way.

5. Give yourself a large reward when you've finally completed your task.

6. Reevaluate your steps and be sure to hone them during your next project. Think of ways you can do things differently or elaborate on things that you know you did right.

7. Get out there and complete your goals!

The next step is to apply the steps and principles that are contained in this book into your life. Also, if you have friends or family members who badly need life transformation, share this book with them. It is my goal to help many people to achieve the life of their dreams.

Finally, if you enjoyed this book, then I'd like to ask you for a favor, would you be kind enough to leave a review for this book on Amazon? It'd be greatly appreciated!

*** FREE BONUS ***

Emotional Intelligence

Develop and apply improved social skills and take control of relationships in your life

Chapter 1:
What Are Emotions?

What Exactly Is An Emotion?

The scientific answer to that would be that an emotional is a psychological state that has three different components: the subjective experience, a physical response, and a behavioral or expressive response.

There are many different ways psychologists have tried to come up with in order to explain emotions. In 1972, a psychologist by the name of Paul Eckman proposed there are six, basic human emotions that are universal. Those emotions include disgust, fear, anger, happiness, surprise and sadness. In 1999, he expanded that list to include excitement, embarrassment, shame, contempt, pride, amusement, and satisfaction.

In between Eckman's times, in the 1980's, Robert Plutchik suggested another classification system. This system was called the wheel of emotions. He suggested there are different emotions that can be combined with one another in order to create another emotion, just like an artist might mix together the primary colors to make another color. Plutchik proposes there are eight primary emotions: happiness, sadness, anger, fear, trust, disgust, surprise, and anticipation. When they are combined, they create another emotion. For example, when happiness and anticipation are combined, they may make excitement.

So what about the three different components of emotions? This may better help you understand your own.

Subjective Experience

Emotions are subjective even though all humans experience the basic, universal emotions. Regardless of our backgrounds or our cultures, we all experience the same basic emotions such as anger, sadness, or happiness. However, our experience of these emotions is actually unique. For example, not all anger is the same. There are subcategories of anger such as mild annoyance all the way up to blinding range.

We never seem to experience a pure form of each emotion, either. Mixed emotions over an even tor a situation your life is not uncommon. Those who are faced with a new job might feel both excited and nervous. Those who are having children or getting married might have anything from joy to anxiety, to all the emotions in between. They can happen at the same time or they may happen one after the other.

Physical Response

You've most likely felt your stomach lurch or twist when you're anxious or your heart palpate with fear. This is a physical response to your emotions. Many of these responses can include sweaty palms, a racing heart, and rapid breathing. These are all part of the sympathetic nervous system, which a branch of the autonomic nervous system. This part of your nervous system controls the body's fight or flight response, and when faced with a threat, these responses prepare your body to flee or face a threat.

Early studies of the physical forms of emotion focused on autonomic response, recent research has targeted the brain's role in your emotions. Brain scans show that the amygdala, a part of your limbic system, has a role in your emotions, especially fear. This is a tiny, almond shaped component of the brain that has been linked to hunger and thirst, as well as emotion and memory.

Behavioral Response

This final component is most likely the one you are most familiar with, the expression of emotions. We spend a lot of time interpreting emotional expressions of those around us, and our ability to accurately understand the expressions of their emotions is what gives us emotional intelligence. These expressions play a large role in our body language. Expressions such as smiling or frowning are universal across the globe.

Our culture also plays a large role in how we express emotions. For example, in Japan, those who are in the presence of an authority figure mask their fear or disgust. They almost seem to shut-down.

Emotions vs. Moods

Did you know that your emotions and moods are actually different? An emotion is something that is short-lived and intense, and they're likely to have a definite and identifiable cause. For example, you may feel angry after an argument with a friend or lover.

A mood is a milder version of an emotion that is longer-lasting. It's usually hard to determine the specific cause of a mood. For example, you may feel sad or lonely for several days without a real reason to feel that way.

Emotions Can Motivate Us to Take Action

Let's say you're facing an exam in the morning that you know is going to be very difficult. What motivates you to study in order to pass that exam? The fear or anxiety you're feeling of failing that important exam. You experienced motivation due to your emotions.

People usually take action in order to experience a positive emotion and minimize their risk of feeling a negative emotion. For example, a person might try to find social activities or hobbies that leave them feel content, happy, and excited. They may also avoid a situation that could lead to sadness, boredom, or anxiety.

Emotions Help Us Survive, Thrive, and Avoid Danger

Darwin believed that emotions were adaptations we developed in order to survive and reproduce. Anger made us confront the source of our irritation, and fear made us flee the threat. Love helped us find mates and seek out reproductions. Emotions are an adaptive role in our lives that motivate us to take action that will maximize chances for success.

Emotions Can Help Us Make Decisions

We may think that our decisions are guided purely by logic and rationality, but our emotions always play a role in our good decision making process. In fact, research on those who have damage to their emotional intelligence shows that they make poor decisions, while those who have good emotional intelligence have excellent decision making skills.

Emotions Allow Other People to Understand Us

Interaction with others is something that happens on a daily basis to us, and it's important that we give them emotional cues to help them understand what we're feeling. These cues can include body language like facial expressions, or stating how we're feeling directly. When we tell someone we're feeling sad, happy, frightened, or excited, we're giving them imperative information that allow them to take action.

Emotions Allow Us to Understand Others

The emotional expression of others around us provides us with a wealth of social information. Communicating socially is an imperative part of our daily lives and relationships, ad when we can interpret and intact with those emotions of others, we're able to build stronger relationships. It allows us to respond in a deeper, more meaningful way that helps us strengthen the bonds with one another.

Darwin was one of the earliest researchers who scientifically studied emotions. He suggested that they are displayed in order for our survival and safety. For example, coming across a hissing or spitting animal tells you the animal is angry and upset. You are more likely to stay away and survive by not getting injured. In addition, we need to be aware of each other's emotions in order to stay out of stressful, dangerous situations and learn how to defuse them successfully.

Chapter 2:
What Is Emotional Intelligence?

What Is Emotional Intelligence?

Your emotional intelligence is your capability to identify, use, understand, and manage your emotions on a positive way to relieve stress, communicate in an effective manner, empathize with those around you, overcome daily challenges, and defuse conflicts. It can impact many different aspects of your life, such as your behavior and how you interact with those around you.

If you have a high emotional intelligence, then you're able to see your emotional state, as well as the emotional state of those around you. You can engage with the people around you and draw them to you rather than push them away. You can use your understanding of their emotions in order to relate to them better, and form healthier relationships. You can also use it to achieve more success at work and lead a more fulfilling life.

Your emotional intelligence has three different attributes. These attributes include:

- Self-awareness: Your ability to see your own emotions and how they're affecting your thoughts, behavior, and actions. It's also your ability to recognize your strengths and weaknesses, and your level of self-confidence.

- Self-manage: This is your ability to control your spontaneous feelings and actions, as well as manage your emotions in a healthy manner. Those who can self-manage can take initiative, complete commitments, and adapt to their circumstances.

- Social awareness: This is your ability to understand the emotions, concerns, and needs of those around you by picking up on their emotional cues, your ability to feel comfortable in a social setting, and how to recognize the dynamics of a group or organization.

Characteristics of Emotional Intelligence

According to Daniel Goleman, there are actually five elements to emotional intelligence. You'll recognize some of these from the previous chapter, but we're going to expand upon them.

Self-awareness

You already know that self-awareness is your ability to understand your own emotions, and that you don't allow your emotions to rule over you. Those who are self-aware are confident individuals because they're able to allow their intuition to take control rather than letting their emotions take control.

Those who have self-awareness first must be able to take an honest look at themselves and know their strengths and weaknesses. They work on those areas in order to perform better.

Most psychologists believe this is the most important part of emotional intelligence.

Self-regulation

When you're able to control your emotions and impulses, you have self-regulation. Those who are able to self-regulate do not allow themselves to become jealous or angry, and they do not ever make carless, impulsive decisions. They are able to think before they act. Some characteristics of this ability to self-regulate include comfort with change, thoughtfulness, integrity, and the ability to say no to others.

Motivation

Motivation plays a key role in having a high degree of emotional intelligence. Those who are motivated are able to defer immediate results for long-term success. They're productive, enjoy a challenge, and are effect in whatever they do.

Empathy

This is considered the second most important part of emotional intelligence. Empathy is your ability to identify with others and understand their needs, wants and viewpoints. Those who have empathy are excellent at recognizing other's feelings, even when they are not obvious. Empathetic people are great at managing relationships, relating to others, and listening. They do not judge quickly and avoid stereotyping others, and they live their lives in an honest and open way.

Social Skills

It's easy to talk with and like people who have excellent social skills, which is another sign of high emotional intelligence. Those who have strong social skills are team players and focus on helping others before they focus on their own success. They manage disputes, communicate effectively, and are masters at relationships.

Why Is Emotional Intelligence So Important?

Emotional intelligence is very important for everyone. We know that those who are the smartest are not always the most successful or the most fulfilled in their lives. We all know someone who is academically brilliant but they're not socially graceful and they're unsuccessful in their work or their personal relationships due to their ineptness. Our intellectual intelligence is not enough for us to be successful and happy in life. Your intellectual intelligence or IQ can get you into college, but your emotional intelligence is what will help you manage your emotions and the stress when you're facing final exams.

So what areas of your life does emotional intelligence affect?

- Work: Your emotional intelligence affects your work life significantly. If you have a high emotional intelligence, you can navigate the social complexities of your workplace and lead or motivate others. You can excel in your career. When it comes to gauging job candidates, companies view emotional intelligence as more important than technical ability and require emotional intelligence testing before they hire candidates.

- Physical Health: Chronic stress is a serious condition for those who are unable to manage their emotions. It leads to some serious health complications such as raised blood pressure, a suppressed immune system, an increased risk of heart attack and stroke, infertility, and a speed up of the aging process. Your first step is going to be learning how to relieve stress if you have a low emotional intelligence, but we'll get to that in later chapters.

- Mental Health: Chronic stress is also very detrimental to your mental health, and makes you vulnerable to illnesses such as anxiety and depression. If you're unable to manage or understand emotions, then you won't be able to manage mood swings. This can lead to the inability to form or manage strong relationships, and this leads to you feeling lonely and isolated.

- Relationships: If you have a stronger emotional intelligence level, then you are able to forge strong relationships with those around you because you can control your emotions and gauge the emotions of those you're speaking with or just being with. This can help you both in your personal and work life.

Chapter 3:
Emotional and Mental Intelligence

What Is Mental Health Or Emotional Health?

Your emotional and mental health refers to your psychological well-being. It includes the quality of your relationships, how you feel about yourself, and your ability to manage your emotions and deal with difficulties in a calm manner.

A good mental health is not just about the absence of mental health problems. It's about being free from anxiety, depression, and other psychological issues. Mental and emotional health refer to positive characteristics. Remember that feeling bad is not the same as feeling good, and while some people may not have negative feelings, they need to do things that make them feel positive in order to feel mental and emotional health.

Those who are mentally and emotionally healthy have:

- A zest for life, laughing and fun.

- A sense of contentment.

- The ability to handle stress and brush past adversity.

- A sense of meaning in their relationships and activities.

- The flexibility to adapt to change and learn new things.

- A balance between their work life, play life, rest, activity, etc.

- The ability to create and maintain a fulfilling relationship with themselves and others.

- High self-esteem and self-confidence.

When you harbor these characteristics of mental and emotional health and stability, you're able to participate in life to the fullest by being productive and having meaningful activities and relationships. When you have these characteristics, you're able to weather life's challenges and stressful moments.

The Role of Resilience in Mental and Emotional Health

When you are emotionally and mentally healthy, it doesn't mean that you don't go through some bad times in your life or experience some emotional problems. Everyone goes through loss, disappointments, and change. They're all normal parts of life that cause anxiety, sadness, and stress.

However, those who have a healthy emotional outlook are able to deal with those moments and bounce back from the trauma, adversity, and stress. This is known as resilience.

People who have tools for coping with those difficult situations and maintain a positive outlook are able to stay focused, creative, and flexible during the bad times, as well as the good.

As aforementioned, one of the key components to having a healthy emotional outlook is being able to balance your stress and your emotions. Your ability to recognize and express your emotions appropriately will help you avoid becoming tuck in anxiety, depression and other negative mood states. You also have to have a strong support network. Being able to trust people and having them around you turns you toward encouragement, which boosts your resilience during those tough times.

Physical Health Is Connected To Mental and Emotional Health

Your body's needs should be of your first concern when it comes to your emotional and mental health. Your mind and your body are linked in a powerful way, and when you improve your physical well-being, you will experience a greater mental and emotional well-being. Exercise strengthens your heart and lungs, and it also releases endorphins that energize and lift your mood.

The activities you perform on a daily basis affect the way you feel emotionally and physically.

Here are some ways to improve your physical health:

- Get rest. When you get enough sleep, seven to eight hours every night, you're able to function with a more clear-headed mind. Without enough sleep, you can develop a short fuse which leads to outbursts.

- Learn about nutrition and practice it. First, do some research on what you should be eating and things you might want to avoid, like excess sugar and processed foods. Then, keep a diary of what you eat on a daily basis and how you feel after you eat those foods for a week. You'll start to see patterns as to what foods might aggravate you and what foods help you stay focused and alert.

- Exercise in order to relieve stress. You don't have to go to a gym in order to boost your endorphins and make yourself mentally happier and healthier. Just take the stairs instead of the elevator or take a walk at lunch for fifteen minutes. Instead of taking the first bus stop, walk to the second one. There are many ways you can add exercise into your daily routine.

- Get some sunlight. You should have ten to fifteen minutes of direct sunlight every day. You can do this while gardening, exercising, or even socializing.

- Limit your alcohol and drug consumption. This includes cigarettes. All of these are stimulants that make you feel good for the short term, but they have some long-term negative side effects for not only your body, but your emotional and mental health, too.

Improve Mental and Emotional Health by Taking Care of Yourself

If you want to maintain and strengthen your emotional and mental health, you have to pay attention to your needs and feelings first. Do not allow stress and negative emotions to build up, but instead try to maintain a balance between your daily responsibilities and the things that make you happy. If you take care of your needs first, you'll be able to deal with challenges when they arise in a much more positive manner.

Taking care of you includes some of the following:

- Do things that positively impact others. When you're being useful to others and being valued for what you're doing, you're building your self-esteem and self-confidence.

- Practice self-discipline. When you practice self-control, this leads to a sense of hopefulness and help you overcome despair.

- Learn to discover something new. Think of discovering something new as intellectual candy. Join a book club, take an adult educational class, learn a new language, visit a museum, or travel somewhere new, even if it's just a town in the same county you live in.

- Enjoy the beauty of art or nature. Studies have shown that those who take the time to smell the roses and view nature are able to lower their blood pressure and reduce their stress. Just sitting on the beach can be a great way to relax your nerves.

- Manage your stress. Stress is our enemy. It used to be necessary for short bursts of time to survive in the wild, but we're not chronically stressed, which can lead to heart disease and many other nasty illnesses. Try taking some stress management classes or utilizing some of the stress relieving tips found later in this book.

- Limit unhealthy habits such as worrying. Stop becoming absorbed in repetitive mental habits, such as negative thoughts about yourself and the world. These drain your energy, suck up your time, and trigger feelings of fear, anxiety, and depression.

- Appeal to your senses. Be sure to remain calm and energized by appealing to your five senses. Listen to music, put some flower on your desk, massages your hands, or drink a warm cup of tea or hot cocoa. Indulge yourself!

- Engage in creative, meaningful work. When you do something that challenges your creativity and makes you feel productive, you boost your confidence and esteem levels. Try something such as writing, gardening, drawing, building something or playing an instrument.

- Get a pet. You're right, they're a big responsibility, but caring for one makes you feel loved and needed. Pets give you unconditional love and they don't care about who you fought with that day or whether or not you forgot the milk. They're always waiting for you when you get home and they're never in a bad mood.

- Make leisure time a priority. Play-time for adults is just as much a necessity as it is for children. We need to engage in leisure time in order to unwind from a hard day at work.

- Make some time for appreciation and contemplation. Think about everything you're grateful for and take some time to meditate, enjoy the sunset, or take a moment to pay attention to what's positive, good and beautiful throughout your day.

Remember that everyone is different and not everything that is good and beneficial to you will be the same for others. Some feel better when they're relaxing while others need stimulation and excitement in order to feel better. Just find the activities in your life that make you feel boosted and energized.

Risk Factors for Mental and Emotional Problems

Mental and emotional health is shaped by experiences. Your early childhood experiences and memories are very significant. Genetic and biological factors may also play a role, but these are usually shaped and changed by experiences, too.

There are some risk factors that are able to compromise your mental and emotional health. These factors include:

- A poor connection or attachment with a primary caretaker in early life. If you felt abused, lonely, isolated, unsafe, or confused as an infant or as a young child, you are at a higher risk for mental and emotional complications.

- Traumas or serious loss, especially earl in life. These might include experiencing a war, hospitalization, or even losing a loved one such as a parent or grandparent.

- Learned helplessness. Sometimes people experience negative experiences that lead to a belief that they're helpless and do not have any control over situations in their life.

- Illness. Chronic or disabling illness that isolates children from others can cause emotional and mental distress.

- Medication side-effects. Those who are older who are taking many medications are more at risk for experiencing side-effects, which can lead to emotional distress.

- Substance abuse. Abusing alcohol and drugs can cause mental, physical, and emotional problems.

Whether you've had internal or external factors that shaped your mental and emotional health, it's not too late to make the necessary changes in order to improve your psychological well-being. These risk factors can be counteracted with protective factors such as a healthy lifestyle, strong relationships, and coping strategies that help you manage stress and your negative emotions.

When to Seek Professional Help for Emotional Problems

Sometimes, no matter how hard we try to do it alone, we need a professional to help us with our mental and emotional health. There's no shame in asking for help, and taking that leap will help you improve greatly.

Some red flag emotions and behaviors include:

- Insomnia

- Feeling helpless and hopeless consistently.

- Having problems concentrating at work and at home.

- Using food, nicotine, drugs, or alcohol in order to cope with your emotions.

- Self-destructive or negative thoughts or fears that you can't seem to control.

- Thoughts of suicide or death.

If you have any of these red flags, then it's best that you seek immediate treatment from a professional.

Chapter 4:
Developing Emotional Intelligence

Do you have emotional intelligence? The truth is that everyone has some level of what is referred to as emotional intelligence – some people just have more of it than others. If you are lacking emotional intelligence, luckily you can learn to develop more of it and use it in your everyday life. But first, how do you know whether you have a lot of emotional intelligence, or only a little? In order to answer this, you will first have to understand what emotional intelligence is.

Emotional intelligence is all about being able to know what people around you are feeling – what their emotions are. People with high emotional intelligence can easily tell what people they are associating with are feeling, and can then use it to benefit both themselves and others. If you understand what others are feeling, you will know how to treat them, talk to them, successfully work with them, and so much more.

You are probably wondering how you can develop your emotional intelligence. Well, you need to try to be more aware of your surroundings. Next time you are around others, try to take in all the little things about them that can signify what they are feeling. Are you someone who is generally caught up in a million things at once? Are you often stressed, worried, and frazzled? If this sounds like you, then you might be having trouble developing emotional intelligence because you don't take the time to focus on what is going on around you - you are always caught up in other things.

To develop your emotional intelligence, try practicing mindfulness. Mindfulness is just focusing on the present – instead of what might happen in the future or what has happened in the past. It sounds so simple, doesn't it? However, the truth is that with all the distractions of life, putting it into practice can be another story entirely.

You will have to work at it – so don't be discouraged if at first you fail. Practice again and again, and you will find yourself getting better at truly living in the present moment. In order to practice mindfulness, it is essential to be calm. So, you may need to do some breathing exercises to get rid of any stress or anxiety. This will hopefully allow you to be calm enough to focus on only what is going on around you, instead of worrying needlessly about other things.

How will this new skill called mindfulness help you develop your emotional intelligence? Well, if you practice mindfulness when you are around others, you will be able to easily pick up on their emotions. You will be focused on the present, which make you a lot less likely to miss a sudden change in, for example, someone's face or voice. It is the little signs like these that can tell you how someone is feeling – and in order to notice them, you need to be completely focused on what is going on around you.

Hopefully these tips will help you develop more emotional intelligence in no time. To quickly summarize the key points of this chapter, be sure to remember how important it is to get rid of stress so you can focus on the present. This will increase your emotional intelligence greatly. But, now that you have greater emotional intelligence, you need to learn how to apply it in everyday life. If correctly applied, emotional intelligence can be extremely helpful. Keep reading to learn how to apply emotional intelligence in your life. Emotional intelligence can help you develop and sustain the relationships you have always wanted. With emotional intelligence, you will have more control over the relationships in your life. If you want to improve a relationship that you feel needs work, you will be able to. If you want to mend a friendship, it won't be as hard. Your family and work life will greatly benefit from your new skill – so don't wait any longer! The next chapter of this book will help you on your journey to improving the relationships in your life.

Conclusion

Being aware of your emotional intelligence levels allows you to branch out further and start educating yourself and practicing with the different techniques that were provided to you in this eBook. Remember that emotional intelligence has nothing to do with your IQ, but it does have everything to do with how people will perceive you and how you will feel about yourself.

Those who have a high emotional intelligence are able to be successful in their personal and business relationships because they are able to understand their spouses, children, and coworkers on a much better level. Just with a few facial expressions, we can convey whether we're sad or happy or if we're just feeling bored. When you're able to read someone's emotions, you'll be able to gauge their reaction to what you're about to say much easier. This could save you a lot of grief and hassle in the future.

So now that you have learned all about emotional intelligence and social skills, emotional intelligence and relationships, how to apply emotional intelligence, and of course, most importantly, how to develop it, the next step is to start putting it into practice in your everyday life. Emotional intelligence can help you greatly in so many situations. No matter how hard a situation may seem, with emotional intelligence it will be easier to get through. Take what you have learned from this book and use it to start living a better life today. It is not hard, and it will definitely be very rewarding!

www.ingramcontent.com/pod-product-compliance
Lightning Source LLC
Chambersburg PA
CBHW070244190526
45169CB00001B/303